CEO SPEAK: LESS

"Real world advice from real experts"

This internationally acclaimed series provides real world lessons from C-level business leaders (CEO, CFO, CTO, CMO, Partner) of some of the world's most respected companies. Each chapter is a future-oriented look at the most important issues for success. Every contributor has been carefully chosen for his or her proven business expertise in order to give readers actual insights from the thoughts, perspectives, and techniques of accomplished professionals worldwide. Because so few books or other publications are actually written by executives in industry, this series presents an unprecedented look at contemporary issues never before available.

"What C-Level executives read to keep their edge and make pivotal business decisions. Timeless classics for indispensable knowledge." Richard Costello, *Marketing Communications, General Electric*

"Want to know what the real leaders are thinking about now? It's in here." Carl Ledbetter, *SVP & CTO, Novell, Inc.*

"Unlike any other business book." Bruce Keller,, *Partner, Debevoise & Plimpton*

"A valuable probe into the thought, perspectives, and techniques of accomplished professionals. By taking a 50,000 foot view, the authors place their endeavours in a context rarely gleaned from text books or treatise."
Chuck Birenbaum, *Partner, Thelen Reid & Priest*

"A great way to see across the changing marketing landscape at a time of significant innovation."
David Kenny, *Chairman & CEO, Digitas*

The Art of Advertising

Top Advertisers Reveal the Secrets of Successful, Creative and Innovative Advertising

VISION BOOKS

(Incorporating Orient Paperbacks)
New Delhi • Mumbai • Hyderabad

www.vision**books**india.com

Authorized edition for sale in the
Indian Sub-continent and South-East Asia

ISBN 81-7094-585-2

Published in 2004 by
Vision Books Pvt. Ltd.
(Incorporating Orient Paperbacks and CARING imprints)
24 Feroze Gandhi Road, Lajpat Nagar-III,
New Delhi-110024, India.

Phone: (+91-11) 2983 6470 ; 2983 6480
Fax: (+91-11) 2983 6490
E-mail: visionbk@vsnl.com

Cover Design by hatchdesign.org

Printed at
Rashtra Rachna Printers
C-88 Ganesh Nagar, Delhi 110092, India.

Contents

Brandtailing™ – Advertising at the Speed of Smart

Jordan Zimmerman

Zimmerman & Partners Advertising

CEO & Chairman

Succeeding in Advertising

Show me a successful client, and I'll show you a successful agency. Success in advertising is connected ultimately to the success of the client. At Zimmerman & Partners Advertising, we embrace that principle. To be successful, you must be involved. You must take the time to learn your client's business and brand attributes well. Let the client know that you care as much about the business as he or she does. Analyze the business, its chief competitors, its unique culture, mission, vision and trends of the category it's in.   Most importantly, stay focused on brand attributes upon which the client can build. Be single minded. Literally. Don't throw many attributes out there in the hope they'll take away just one. Be certain the one is the one you want them to take away. If you don't know your client's business intimately, you are likely to focus on attributes that really aren't important to the consumer, often at the client's request. It's your uncomfortable obligation to be honest and say, "That's an attribute that has no meaning to the consumer." Recommend what is right for the business, what is supported by logic, research and solid, strategic thinking; that which differentiates your brand from the competition. Only then can you communicate in a compelling manner. Only then can you cut through the clutter and attract the interest and attention the client needs to grow its business. For more than 25 years, this has been my strategy for success.

Five not-so-easy pieces to success

There are five essential skill sets in advertising. The first is accountability. The bar is set with the client's business objectives. Then we raise it a few notches higher. Our philosophy is that image-building and branding must always be balanced against the need to deliver on the bottom line. Advertising is a means to an end, not an end in itself. Successful clients make the best clients; we want to create brand leaders—clients with skyrocketing sales and sparkling creative.

The second essential skill is media savvy. With media fragmentation increasing exponentially, each medium must be understood for what it is really capable of delivering. It must be targeted precisely and assessed with the end user in mind. As with creative, media planning and placement must build the client's business.

The third essential skill is unyielding commitment. You are more than the agency; you must be an evangelist, preaching the virtues of your client to your staff, your client's staff and the public. We must be committed advocates as well as dedicated business partners. The entrepreneurial approach that we apply to each of our clients' businesses must be evident in every phase of the advertising development, from planning to creative to execution. No task is too big and, equally important, no job too small. It is also crucial to be proactive. It is essential to deliver more than what the client asks for.

The fourth essential skill is to be disciplined. At Zimmerman & Partners, we assist clients in focusing on the compelling, differentiating selling points that induce consumer consideration. We must never lose sight of that focus as we move from creative development through media planning and execution. We seek to reach targeted consumers with an effective, focused communication to which they will respond. Say one thing. Say it well. Say it often.

The fifth essential skill is creativity, the art of being inventive and imaginative. We must apply creativity to everything we do—tirelessly exploring innovative ways to communicate the brand selling point in a meaningful, relevant way. A message has to break through and resonate with the consumer to be successful. Consumers are not waiting for your message. You must deliver it to them in an unexpected manner. Creative has an aftershock. It will be felt long after it stops running. When that happens, you've done your job. That's creativity you can't put a price on.

Advertising and Branding

Advertising allows you to communicate a salient message to a large group of consumers faster than any other form of communication. It allows you to truly connect with the consumer; it gives you an opportunity to develop an ongoing relationship between the consumer and a brand. At its best, advertising will create a sense of urgency for the consumer, an awareness—often honest and accurate—that there are products, places, styles or sensibilities that cry out for action or attention.

Breakthrough ideas might appear to be instant or impulsive, but they are not. They are based on sound strategy, outstanding visuals and copy, and the correct application of timing and media. The art is in ensuring that all elements of communication work together so that the end result is more powerful and effective. It's like conducting a symphony orchestra—all the instruments working together, the timing just right to make beautiful music. In the world of advertising, this is a total business solution. We don't see ourselves as an "advertising" agency. We're the conductors helping orchestrate a business success.

There are various styles of advertising—a soft sell or a hard sell, a subtle approach or a blatant approach, an informative style or a modern and edgy one. Style will always change: with the product or service you are selling; with the timing of the message; with the medium you are using. Style will also be influenced by the life stage of the brand. You can use different styles of advertising with a mature brand like Coca-Cola, more than you can with a new brand or one that is declining or has lost its way. The important thing is finding the right balance between defining a brand and delivering next-day sales. The true craft is in identifying ways to interest consumers in what is being offered. A creative strategy can put you on the right course, but in a world filled with clutter and distractions you must develop communications that capture consumer attention and interest. The key is delivering the selling point in an interesting, single-minded, non-contrived manner. Some advertising sells brands. Great advertising also builds them.

Assuming a client's product or service meets an immediate or unfulfilled future need, it must deliver on three or four attributes differentiating it from whatever else is out there. Let's take our client Nissan as an example. Nissan sells a basic commodity: cars. However, Nissan not only delivers exceptional value, it understands how to differentiate itself from the competition, employing persuasive messaging that hits at the core audience's relevant needs. However, there is another level of understanding here: Nissan is smart about building cars because it understands through relevant research what potential customers need and what they want. At Zimmerman & Partners, it's our job to identify those core attributes—match them with consumer desire and bring them to life in our advertising and marketing campaigns. As a result, during the consumer's consideration process, Nissan ranks high on the shopping list. We know what triggers a consumer's desire beyond price point alone. We don't want to get caught up in a price game; like Nissan, we must be strategically smarter than that by promoting exceptional quality at affordable prices—advertising to both the heart and the mind.

Once a brand's core attributes are defined, the message must be communicated to generate customer awareness—a message that incorporates the basic tenets of the brand promise: quality, price, customer-service and follow-up. This must all be done on a consistent basis with the long term in mind. Great brands are not fads. A great brand is just that—a brand that understands how to differentiate itself and become a consumer presence.

Today, discipline in advertising is vitally important because of the intensely competitive environment and the need for immediate results. Discipline means being true to a brand's strategy and staying focused. Too often we see advertising that is so off strategically it does irreparable harm to a brand. Often this happens because a concept perceived as "exciting" or "breakthrough" is actually confusing, unfocused and lacking in clarity. The brand loses its way and its potential customers because of a lack of discipline. We believe that if we understand and define what a brand stands for, who the consumers are, and what key attributes they are seeking, we will always be on strategy.

Of course, for a brand to break through, it must meet a valid, relevant consumer need. The message then must be focused and single-minded, so that the consumer takeaway is clear and distinct. Second, there must be enough of the right message delivered to the right target audience in the right medium to be remembered. The products or service must deliver on the promise.

Great brands have the ability to manifest themselves through different styles and different copy points as long as the brand's core message is consistent. In a highly fragmented market with highly targeted media—specialty publications, cable television, or specific-format radio stations —we can deliver different styles of messaging to the marketplace and lessen the risk of sending a mixed message. The trouble starts when the product does not deliver on the attributes communicated or when the attributes are far removed from how the product is perceived in the marketplace. At Zimmerman & Partners we never sacrifice clarity for the sake of style or execution.

However, it's our experience that the core component of the brand message must contain some specific, consistent elements. For example, we have been instrumental in helping one of our clients, Lennar Homes, build on its concept called EI – Everything's Included. Consumers are often frustrated walking into new homes that are absolutely gorgeous, deciding to buy one, then discovering that everything in the model is an expensive upgrade. Our idea with Lennar Homes was to give them a point of differentiation: When you walk into the model, what you see is what you get. It's affordable. Wall Street loved the idea, and analysts said EI was one of the most successful concepts in the housing category. You walk into a Lennar home and everything's included, but you also get top-quality merchandise instead of having to upgrade it yourself, incurring that incremental cost. The house might be a little more expensive, but ultimately you're getting more value. This has proven quite successful for Lennar Homes: They're a leading homebuilder in the United States today and a Wall Street darling. Their stock has continued to grow, even in these risky times. It's all due to differentiating themselves with a concept that reaches consumers in their hearts, their minds, and most importantly their pockets—a "value" story that was most valuable to Lennar.

In my opinion, it is significantly harder to achieve this kind of breakthrough today. Sectors are busier, and substitutes and competitors can come to market faster today than in the past—so fast, it's almost scary. The proliferation of media options requires a smarter approach today than it did just a few years ago. Think about it: We used to have three networks, ABC, CBS, and NBC. Today the range of options, given cable and satellite television, is unbelievable. There used to be a few key publications, radio, and no online media. Today everything is coming at you. In the wrong hands, multi-media can dilute a message. In the right hands, you can hammer it home.

Growing or Killing a Brand

It is important to understand the life cycle of a category, a brand, and a product to take a brand to the next level and drive long-term success. New brands must establish a niche. A mature brand must find new life, possibly by reinventing itself through extensions or by creating a new identity that connects with today's consumers. Finding more core customers or finding new customers for the brand are challenges that require different approaches. Building on your strengths with customers who truly like and need your product is easier than developing a new customer group. It is mandatory to constantly refresh your consumer data and research to keep up with the trends. Things are moving faster today than ever before; consumers are smarter than ever.

While finding new customer segments, there is always the challenge of not offending current customers while building the brand with the new target group that may have different core needs and require a different advertising approach. For example, Oldsmobile had a longtime hold on its market segment. The market inevitably became older and older. At that time, Oldsmobile decided to run a "This is not your father's Oldsmobile" campaign. What happened? Not only did it not attract a new audience, it turned off its core audience. The result, Oldsmobile declined as a brand.

We have a handful of brands around today that will stand the test of time. Coke is one. Ford might be another, but it will take some luck, some very smart brand and business management, and no crisis situations. Who would have thought Arthur Andersen would disappear? Who could have foreseen the Goodyear tire fiasco with the Ford Explorer? Brands must be nimble; their stewards must know how to evolve and have the commitment to make the changes necessary to continue to be great. It is important to react quickly, but you must move at the "speed of smart."

Typically, what kills an established brand is bad management, lack of foresight and vision—stewards who have become complacent and don't take risks or have allowed the product to lose its connection to the consumer. Bad product, marketing or pricing decisions can kill a brand over time.

Environmental and ethical issues can kill a brand overnight. A discontinuity will kill a brand today. No one knows what unfulfilled need is around the corner that will allow consumers to substitute one product for another. Tic Tacs appeared and eroded Dentyne's market share overnight. Dentyne never saw it coming.

If some of a brand's core attributes have become less relevant to today's consumer, then a brand will have to reinvent itself to survive and grow. It is usually a tougher challenge to invent a new brand completely. If a brand has a strong but eroding foundation, it has a base to build on. Evolving a brand doesn't necessarily mean a complete reinvention. Budweiser is a good example of a brand staying fresh in its approach without constantly reinventing itself.

Advertising Pitfalls

There are four main pitfalls in advertising. The first is strategic: a lack of strategic foundation and focus; a mismatch of target and product; a bland, vanilla positioning platform; a lack of differentiation and a lack of relevance. It's just like life: It's good to know what you want to say before you open your mouth.

There are creative pitfalls. These include trying to communicate too many attributes that mean little to the consumer, which, in a sense, is a strategic shortcoming. There's playing it safe. Safe is not what makes great brands.

Safe is not what inspires consumers to buy great brands. Safe is not where we as advertising agencies want to be. Safe won't change anything. There's lack of style, interest, and the hard to define ability to cut through clutter. If you don't have style in your advertising, it isn't interesting, it can't cut through clutter, and you are wasting your client's dollar. Your client, by the way, should look for a new agency.

Third, there are media pitfalls—especially spending too thinly. We talk a lot about frequency. We are hit with thousands of different messages every day. How can we respond? Frequency is the future of advertising and marketing. Spreading yourself too thinly prevents you from having the kind of frequency you need to drive sales. It's inefficient spending. Media that whispers isn't heard. If you don't have many dollars to spend, don't spread them too thinly. Instead, spend in appropriate channels. If we're not effective in our targeting, we're won't be effective in delivering the results for the client. The most creative, compelling message is useless if nobody is hearing or seeing it.

Finally, there are measurement pitfalls: Measurement tools are not in place, realistic yet achievable goals are not set, an audit is not completed. You have to know what's working and what's not working. At Zimmerman & Partners, we have designed proprietary programs such as Ztrac, a real time Internet-based platform that tracks traditional medias and enables us to monitor our client's progress. Ultimately, successful advertising is like a journey: You need a map to arrive at a destination; you need markers, warning of detours and impassable roads. Without measurement, there are no markers, nothing to direct you to your destination or warn you of the cliff up ahead. Stay aggressive. There should always be a set goal—but never a finish line.

Budgeting and ROI

We work with large budgets, small ones, and others in the middle. The secret in making a budget work is resource allocation: Focus on those areas that have the greatest efficiencies and effectiveness given the size of the budget you have. If you have the resources, a truly integrated approach allows you to be persuasive with the message and to hit your target customers whomever, whenever and wherever they may be. You can spend money on extensive research and preparing to deliver your message. You can put the right systems and processes in place to effectively track and measure the advertising. You can set a true customer relationship management program in place and have the time to get it right through testing and refinement. Having the ability to use interactive media allows you to be ahead of the curve before your competitors have a chance to either understand or test these approaches themselves. I believe that if you have the time and the money, anything can be accomplished because you can lead yourself strategically from the beginning to the end with very little risk. But always remember, having all the money in the world and simply throwing it at a problem will not solve it—you still have to aim.

If spending is a factor, radio is an extremely effective tool. The key with smaller budgets is to focus, prioritize, and not try to do too much. All too often we see clients with very small budgets who want to compete against companies with much larger market share. Copycatting is not an effective tactic for penetrating a market, particularly with a small budget. Often, however, you can break through using radio, a medium that has not been used effectively even by the bigger ad agencies. Radio is highly effective on a cost-per-point basis. Most importantly, it works and is a good responsive medium. Some reasons: drive times in the United States have not become shorter; they've become longer. People have become more infatuated with radio/traffic reports/news bulletins than ever before, and offer a captive audience. Our job is to have an effective communication strategy to break through on the radio.

At Zimmerman & Partners, we measure return on investment through sales, sales, sales. The questions to ask are: Did the cash register ring? Did we deliver sales revenue in an affordable and profitable way? Did we deliver market share? Did we become the talk and the preference? If we did, then we were successful on all fronts.

A successful advertising campaign accomplishes the stated objectives and beats them. Objectives are set, measurement parameters are defined, and a campaign is developed, launched, and measured accordingly. Intuitively, a successful campaign is one that effectively reaches target audiences in a memorable, compelling way and motivates them to act with immediacy. We don't have time to wait for them to act. What we do must inspire them to act now. We must hit at the heartstrings, i.e. forge an emotional connection, with the products we're moving. Advertising is not entertainment; it is a sales tool.

The old adage of whether the cup is half full or half empty no longer holds in today's business climate. Our clients are demanding—their advertising must work, and it must work now. They don't have the time or the marketing dollars to waste waiting for a marketing message to sink in and then wait even longer for it to eventually drive sales. It is all about accountability, more so than ever before in our industry. I like it. It's more fun, more challenging, and at the same time you see your results enhance your own bottom line.

Ultimately, it all comes back to the client. We always have to keep the best interests of the client in mind. It isn't about the agency. It isn't about winning awards. It's about our client's business. They hired us as an advertising agency to do one thing: to help their business, to grow their brand strategically. So we need to learn to manage their budgets and spend their money like it is our own. Then we need to measure results, as much as we monitor our own return on investment. If we are not achieving the results, we need to learn why and not make that same mistake again. The bottom line is that it all comes down to their bottom line, period. End of story.

The necessity of accountability will continue to strengthen until it becomes top-of-mind for agencies and clients. More and more agencies will have to quantify the impact they are having on their clients' businesses. They will have to illustrate specifically how advertising initiatives are advancing company goals. Simply creating ads will not be enough for agencies to succeed. Agencies will need to go further and develop nontraditional ways to grow clients' businesses. This includes delivering alternative marketing initiatives and providing strategic insight on how clients can grow and run their businesses, be it through line extensions, acquisitions, or distribution channel expansion. Agencies need to show they are valuable business partners that share clients' goals rather than pursue their own goals as agencies. They need to show they are true strategic partners present every step of the way, giving their clients guidance and a view from outside their networks. Smart clients and confident agencies will tie compensation programs directly to results.

Changes in the Industry

Five years ago, many people saw the Internet and technology as the future of selling. What we've learned is that the consumer has used it to be more informed and educated, to make more of a rational decision about the products or services he or she wants to buy. It allows advertisers to interact with end users in the privacy of their homes or offices and on their own timetables. It allows us to track quickly the dynamics of fast-changing markets and to react on our clients' behalves. It allows us to track and measure the effectiveness of our advertising campaigns in real time.

The Internet will continue to grow and be important in some industries and with some products and brands. Technology will continue to evolve, and we'll use those innovations that make us more productive and effective in what we do. However, using technology just for the sake of being leading edge is counterproductive. Like strong creative, technology is a tool, not an end in itself.

Technology is an enabler throughout all stages of the advertising process, from creative development to the delivery of advertising to measurement and tracking. Technology has changed the speed and quality of the advertising we deliver. For example, we can now record—in our studios—voice or music talent from around the world to be used in our commercials. At Zimmerman & Partners, we house our own studios so we can do it better, faster, and more affordably for our clients. We can record a saxophone player in Los Angeles, voice talent in Detroit, and somebody else in Europe all at the same time with digital quality. It's become part of the dynamic world we live in today. Technology allows us to react, to make changes in our work in a matter of minutes rather than days.

Broadband is a so-called disruptive technology from an advertising perspective, i.e. it will interrupt or dramatically change the way we do things. It will become, among other things, the fourth pillar of the media world. It plays a role in advertising on demand. Other upcoming applications of technology include animation and robotics. Animation is not currently at a cost-effective stage and is not realistic enough to use extensively in commercials in place of human talent. Robotics will one day allow us to shoot TV commercials in places we could never go, or do things we can only imagine.

In the future, advertising will become even more persuasive and also optional. Consumers will be able to shut out irrelevant or incomprehensible messages. We'll be given more opportunities to accept only messages we want to receive, whether broadcast or online. We will also be able to program the types of ads we want. At some future point, the agency will need to target carefully and make sure messages are clear, relevant, and desirable to audiences, knowing that they will be able to pick and choose.

In the next few years, advertising will be faster, higher quality, and more targeted. True one-on-one marketing means a different message communicated to every consumer. We'll move ever closer to that, which means advertising executives will have to stay on top of their game—and everyone else's game—that much more.

Advertising is a fun, but challenging business. Today the consumer wants more and more; that need must be served, as every market sector becomes more competitive. There were four or so brands in the automotive sector in 1956. Today there are more than 30 brands and the same is true in other sectors. It is extremely difficult to be dominant: You have to be smart to be the best in a splintered market. Clients won't stay for the wrong reasons. The brand is the lifeblood of any corporation. It is up to the adverting agency to grow, defend, and support its promise.

Jordan Zimmerman is the founder, CEO and Chairman of the board of Zimmerman & Partners Advertising.

At age eight he started the only greeting card sales route in New Jersey and for the next three years went door-to-door selling "good wishes" and "holiday cheer." He sold the venture at age 11, turning his first profit.

During his senior year of college, Zimmerman recognized the true power of words when a girl in a focus group on drug abuse responded with, "I just say no." Consequently, he led the "Just Say No" marketing initiative during the Carter Administration (one of the most recognizable anti-drug campaigns to date).

Today, his advertising agency is one of the largest and most successful in the United States. Coining the phrase "Brandtailing," Zimmerman effectively merged the elements of branding and retailing to develop an advertising discipline that creates positive long-term brand identity, as well as short-term retail results.

Breakthrough Advertising:

A Mix of Science & Art

Ernest W. Bromley

Bromley Communications

Chairman & CEO

The Art of Advertising

Advertising is a mix of science and art. Most companies approach marketing problems in the same way – we all do a certain level of copy testing, using qualitative and/or quantitative research techniques. That is the science side of it. The art is in the ideas. It's in being able to see something that others don't see and to develop creative ideas around it. There's a lot of art to that. It's not just something you can wake up one morning and do.

There are some fundamental rules which successful advertising must follow. First, you need to understand the brand you're about to take on. Ask questions such as: What are its core equities? Who are the brand's consumers? From there, you need to understand the consumers and observe how that brand fits into their lives and their day-to-day routines. Once you've got that, you can develop a strong, critical consumer insight. Then marry that insight with the core equities of the brand. That way the insight becomes brand-centric. After that, you provide a strong creative brief that helps the creative understand the brand, the barriers the brand might face, and exactly what it is that the advertising should do.

In reviewing the creative's ideas, it is important that you keep in mind whether they really deliver on the marketing strategy. You need to set aside your own tastes and put yourself in the consumer's shoes, because nine times out of 10 you aren't the target consumer anyway. Ask, "Will this idea connect to the consumer?" Once you've completed your review, take the ideas to the client. You have to listen to the client, because its job is to protect the core equities of the brand. The client needs to feel comfortable, but also needs to judge the idea the way you did – will it connect? You need to cut through the clutter, engage the consumers, and persuade them to take an action or purchase the product. At the end of the process, you need to get the results and learn from them. Don't be disheartened if the results are negative: Understand what went wrong. If the process worked well, understand what made it successful and keep it going.

To succeed in the advertising business, you must be able to see opportunity in the abstract and then, you must make it real. From there, you develop creative ideas that will serve as vehicles to communicate and generate a response.

To be a really good creative, you have to experience a lot of things – read a lot, see a lot of movies, talk to a lot of people. When you start to think out solutions, it's really a subset of your experiences. You need to be someone with a wide range of experiences and who finds it easy to come up with creative ideas or solutions to problems. This is very hard work, but the people who are really creative make it seem simple. A lot of people burn out; coming up with a fresh idea every day is tough. To do it for years, there has to be a level of passion and love.

You also have to stay on top of the industry. I do this by attending seminars. We review creative work done by our competition, which is available on the Internet. We're constantly reading up on what's happening in the industry through trade publications, as well as our clients' trade publications. We're forever students. If you don't remain a student, you'll go out of business. Learning can't stop.

Breaking Through

Good breakthrough advertising has a moment of pure magic to it. It finds a way to engage the target consumer. One key to doing this is by generating some cleverness in the ad. It can come in any number of ways – through drama, humor, the use of music, offering a slice of life, or some sort of technological special effects.

The client is a key part of this process. A campaign can't be truly successful unless the client understands the process and becomes a partner in it. The client also needs to be willing to take a few risks, to approach the market in fresh ways. If a client is very averse to risk, they should expect the same results they've been getting for the past few years. A fair amount of risk taking is necessary. It takes research to convince a skeptical client that this creative idea could resonate with consumers. Research gives the project a good sense of direction and helps people feel they have a solid idea worth taking to consumers. It helps minimize risks for both the client and the agency.

A new campaign, however, isn't without its challenges. The biggest challenge is to fully understand the brand, its core equities, the consumer, and where the brand ranks with that consumer. You have to get the brand to fit within the consumer's cycle. Determining where the brand resides in the consumer's life requires primary research.

Pitfalls in this work stem from failing to complete the proper research and prep work to fully understand the consumer. When you put together an image and you don't understand what the consumer thinks, you put out an image that's not based on reality. The consumer will see right through it, and that message won't be persuasive. The result: People will not buy the brand, the client gets upset, and you get fired.

When a strategy is executed correctly, a brand can survive forever, but it still needs to grow with the consumer base. It can't mean the same thing forever. People's lives change, so a brand needs to evolve, or it will seem like yesterday's brand. Take Coca-Cola, for example. There was a time when the brand was product-driven: It was described as being delicious and refreshing. But today it's very much an icon brand. It's in the fabric of our communities as a leader brand. It has worked hard to be in tune with young people, because that's the group that drinks soda. But that group evolves – how 17-year-olds look in 2003 is very different from how they looked in 1973. Coke has been able to evolve the brand consistently. It takes commitment for a brand to live forever, and it's not cheap to make it happen.

Keeping a brand fresh over the years has become more difficult. There's a lot of clutter – so many brands. It's a continuous challenge to keep a brand fresh. The competition is fiercer than ever. That's one reason why it's important to have a consistent message in all media. Consider how media is fragmenting – cable channels, satellite dishes, the Internet, the wide variety of print vehicles. Whether online or offline, consumers can be reached through many different touch-points. So it's important to provide strategic communication that's consistent across all media vehicles. You're trying to establish frequency, and the consumer is more likely to do what you're telling them to do if they see the same message in different places.

For me, the most exciting part of this industry is trying to understand a problem a brand is facing and then building that brand. We analyze a lot of data then develop a brief on which our creative people can base ideas. When those ideas actually work and we see sales increase, it is a gratifying experience. That's the reward for most of the people in our company.

A Changing Industry

Beyond just being a new media vehicle, the Internet has affected our business in many different ways. For example, we've used the Internet for doing casting calls rather than traveling. We do the casting calls in different markets and then review them from our office. We can get stock photos, many for free, from the Internet. If we need competitive information, we can get it on the Web. Having that information is really good in such a competitive industry. The tools the Internet has afforded to the business are practically unlimited. The Internet's only negative impact is that some of us pushed clients into it, but it didn't deliver the results we expected. So now we're all looking at it with a critical eye. A few years ago, nobody was looking at business models. There were a lot of sites out there that got hits, but they weren't quality hits. We've all learned from that.

Over the last 18 years, the backside of the industry has changed. We've gone from sending things with old fax machines to overnight FedEx to better fax machines to e-mail and the Internet. Everything is fast. We still produce commercials, but today they're done on computer instead of being developed on drawing boards. The technology side of our business has changed so much over the last 20 years, and it will be even more fundamental to our success in the future.

Television has gone digital. As the Internet flourishes with it, the notion of a 30-second commercial becomes obsolete. I see us developing five-minute stories available on Web sites as a way of selling complicated products such as cars. On the BMW website, they show mini-dramas. They're not expensively produced – they probably cost as much as a well-produced 30-second spot – but the consumer can see the product in a real-life situation and get more information on the car right there. That aspect of our business is going to change dramatically.

Advertising has an interesting mix of marketing science along with a sense of Hollywood. It's an industry where you can see marketing problems and develop video or film stories done in 30-second bites. It's a unique and competitive business. It's not for everybody: It's for someone who enjoys a fast pace and can see a project through to a rewarding end. It's a special business and it all comes back to the research – the science, the art, the creativity.

Ernest W. Bromley was part of the original team that founded Bromley Communications in 1981. Throughout his career at the agency, he has worn many hats -- earning a series of promotions ranging from director of research, executive vice president, and president, Bromley now serves as Chairman/CEO of Bromley Communications. Responsible for development and execution of the agency's vision and outstanding products and services, Bromley works closely with account teams in developing sound marketing strategies for the firm's clients. Bromley has also been instrumental in developing the agency's research and Hispanic marketing approach, AIG (Acculturation Influence Groups). This principle of segmenting the Hispanic consumer into levels of language and culture comfort zones is widely utilized by the industry.

Bromley has been a trailblazer in building the agency to be the leading Hispanic marketing communications company, empowering clients such as Procter & Gamble, Burger King, The American Legacy Foundation, and Payless ShoeSource, in the changing American marketplace.

Prior to joining the agency, Bromley taught economics at the University of Texas at San Antonio. He has a bachelor of arts in political science, and a master's in business administration from the University of Texas at San Antonio.

An active community and civic leader, Bromley currently serves as incoming chair for the KLRN Alamo Public Telecommunications Council board of directors, the Free Trade Alliance, AVANCE, Christus Health Futures Task Force, the Advertising Forum of The University of Texas at Austin School of Advertising, The University of Texas at San Antonio College of Business Advisory Council, and the Southwest School of Art and Craft.

A Few True Golden Rules: Keep Current, Be Curious, Never Stop Listening

G. Steven Dapper

Hawkeye Worldwide Communications

Founder, Chairman

Advertising – What It Takes

I have a fairly broad definition of what I believe advertising is. To me, it's a compendium of all communications that a consumer sees, feels, touches, hears, smells, and so on. If they're walking through a store, the packaging on a particular product is advertising. If they are at home, the direct mail they receive in their mailbox, the e-mails and pop-ups on their computers, or the images they see on television are advertising. The logos on the NASCAR autos or even the t-shirts with every name known to mankind are advertising.

I do not believe there are any specific golden rules for successful advertising. I think whatever rules do exist should be broken, because once you set them down on paper and decide to follow them every time, you create the same vanilla message over and over again. So I suppose that means the true golden rule is to keep changing, keep searching for that original thought, and never forget that the brand has to be successful for you to be successful. Whatever tool is needed to move the product and brand should be explored, whether you're on the client side or the agency side.

It's also important to stay current regarding the world around you. For me, it helps to have two young daughters and to have followed them through their teenage years, observing what they and their friends are doing. I think you need to experience going to the theater, the ballet, taking trips out to Iowa, journeying to a farm community, going bowling in Kansas, venturing to Australia, or Cartegena, reading everything you can. You can't shut down to the new things going on in life.

The essential skills for success in advertising include being eclectic and covering different types of ground, because being curious about the world is probably one of the best traits that anyone can have if you want to succeed in marketing and advertising. You must passionately try to understand why people do things, what triggers them to make their purchase decisions, how they use these products after purchasing, and always have empathy for people who like different things than you do.

Being inquisitive about the world and how it works is extremely important for success in advertising from a communications standpoint, but it takes common sense, passion, and the ability to deal rationally with others to get your ideas sold. In the end, everything that gets produced is a team effort, and there must be that passion about wanting to do things right.

Advertising is a fine balance between art and science. The science part of it is consuming information, but the true challenge is translating these facts into a relevant strategy, into an original, creative execution, and generating the right communication stream. I passionately believe that the physical, creative part of what we do is an art, an exceptionally true craft. An individual sitting down with a blank piece of paper and coming up with an idea, a look, a feel, a word that captures the essence of what that brand means to a consumer or what problem it solves' for the consumer is able to do so because it is inherent within them. It can be structured and certainly nurtured, but it can never be completely taught. There is something in a soul that allows you to create wonderful, effective advertising.

It is a group of individuals that the world sometimes believes to be too quirky. Some of the most disciplined people I've ever met in the advertising business comprise the creative talent. You must study a lot of things, you have a time frame, you have to shoot a commercial, you have to set type, and you have to get something produced for it to have an effect on the consumer. I think people set pretty good timetables for themselves. However, they may run by their own clocks. The good thing about advertising and being disciplined is that there are so many ways to get to that end solution, and advertising has been great in not dictating how people have to work or dress as long as you can get to that end result on time. If it works, go ahead and do it.

The one crucial element in advertising is to never stop listening. Keep looking at the entire world and what goes on in it. Change is all around you, and if you stop noticing it, you're dead. Coming out of college, I almost took a job at the Federal Reserve Bank in Chicago. A recruiter said would be a big mistake to go into the unstable advertising world. It would be too unpredictable. Well, I'm glad I kept going on Interstate 80 to Madison Avenue. It has been and is a fascinating experience and the banking industry doesn't appear to be that stable of late!

Executing the Campaign

To build a brand, you first must have a great product with good distribution. The quickest death for a bad product is good advertising, because people try it and never come back to it. It takes having a great product, then developing the trust and belief of brand managers or senior-level clients who allow you to create the communication and adver sing that can make a difference in the marketplace. You need advertising that can take the product out of the commodity decision cycle and make it a very real, personal choice with tangible benefits for the consumer.

To break through, your communication must be relevant. It has to be memorable in some way, and that doesn't mean crazy or loud, but it should hit a specific part of the consumer's psyche. Consumers should say, "Wow, I didn't know that about that brand," or "Wow, that brand really does something for me or says something about me," or "That brand is something we need."

Having one consistent message through all forms of media is a good mantra to follow. Consumers are very smart, and if you confuse them, or try to fool them, they're going to make a different choice about your brand. The consumer must always be handled with a healthy dose of respect. The idea of integration of message and brand essence is very important. Whether it all has to come from one agency is disputable, but from a brand or client perspective everything they produce should have the brand's essence and positioning within it.

Even if it's just a sale with an extra 10 percent off on Saturday, it must still say something solid about the store or the product.

A product's sustainability can bring an advertising campaign to life. There have been lots of executions that people thought were different, or cute, or really caught your attention right away through fresh, original concepts, but over time a campaign, a brand, has to be sustainable. You want to be able to nurture and massage that communication stream over time. Without that, you have too many tactical executions that may have little blips of sales, but are very difficult to sustain preference.

We're a very visual audience. The world is changing in so many ways. Television shows and movies are quickly clipped, with constant talking and constant cuts. There are no more long, drifting scenes. You must understand that this is how people consume information. You must work to bring them in, but then your campaign must nurture them along and be there for a long time.

There are some major pitfalls to avoid in any advertising campaign. First, always refrain from using the word "I," because a team gets you there. Never be reluctant to embrace a person who can help you get to the end result.

Next, never show arrogance or disrespect in your campaign, because it will turn too many consumers away from the brand.

Another pitfall is failing to listen and adjust. You must stop and see the reality of the world around you.

Finally, have a high degree of well-placed confidence. Rejection will happen, whether from the client or the consumer.

Ultimately, a successful advertising campaign solves the problem the brand is facing in the marketplace. The product or brand moves in the marketplace, and the advertising effort has either helped it to grow or stopped the erosion of sales. If the brand is declining, how do you stop that from happening, and how do you help move the brand? Things like that are very important in determining whether an advertising campaign is a success or failure.

Evolution

Initial success in a campaign doesn't mean you put your feet up. Brands are like human beings, and they constantly have to be evolved, refreshed and loved. You definitely must stay true to who you are, but it doesn't hurt to buy a new jacket and cowboy boots and dance a little jig once in a while. It definitely will pay to have a sixth sense about what's going on in the world around you and how the brand fits into the constantly evolving consumer. There should not be one vanilla description of the consumer. Your franchise is comprised of hundreds of segments that see and use your brand for a myriad of reasons. This is to keep the brand fresh.

You have to stay close to the consumer. Certain companies, such as Pepsi, Coke, Nike, or BMW, are great marketing companies. They constantly try to evolve or have brand extensions, but they stay on solid ground for what their DNA was intended to be. They change based on consumer wants, needs or mores, and that is essential to garner continued success.

Reinvention, or evolution, has become much harder in recent times, because the world is becoming harder to live in. It's much more global with constant information bursts and choices. Plus, life is not made easier with so many accountants involved in leading brands and creating advertising. They try to make a formula of it: "All right, you have seven hours to come up with an idea!" I believe most people who practice this craft understand you must make a profit on the bottom line, but you cannot put the value of a big idea into a spreadsheet. The craft we all try to practice has to be rejuvenated by taking a calculated risk here and there to keep everything moving forward. The economy is hurting not only here but in the United Kingdom and throughout the world, yet pressure from Wall Street demands 15-20 percent increases to hold your stock price. They're putting marketing managers at odds, undermining what's best for long-term brand performance, and most importantly pitting the consumer against the shareholder.

Because of terrorism, September 11, and the war in Iraq, we have increased devotion to, and renewed love of, family, friends and values. A little ethics can go a long way if practiced, not just discussed over cigars, and communications must understand this human essence. People want good songs, memorable, vibrant visuals, and relevant copy. We all have to keep living and moving forward, so communications must be strong and bold but aware of where the consumer is and for the world we live in.

Some would hope a brand could live forever. I believe a brand can keep going as long as there's a need for it and as long as it's fresh. Brands die when there's no longer a use for them. The communication has become stilted, or has been untruthful, or the brand promise was fictitious. Consumers are a very smart group. They don't love people or brands that annoy them or bring them false hope.

The Business of Advertising

Risk is a significant part of advertising, and the range from playing it too safe to taking calculated risks to just winging it is wide. You have to go with what's in your heart and soul. Advertising has become way too safe. It's not as bold or as much fun as it used to be. That is not the fault only of those at the agency; it is also driven by people on the client side who don't want to take a short term risk or assume their MBAs gives them a world of experience.

Evaluating risk is very difficult. To suggest and try change, you must be prepared to be rejected at times, because people really do not want to change. You have to study the palate from left to right, the individual rainbow of color you can choose from to describe life. Sometimes it's best to take a wide swatch quickly, try something new and different, and see if it works. But, you also must have the ability and guts to admit it's not working and make the necessary adjustments or kill the campaign or product.

Advertising will always be dependant on a brand's budget to some degree. Having inadequate money to spend, puts undo pressure on the advertising. Whether you have the budget or not, the advertising must be truthful, relevant, eye catching, memorable and down right pleasing. It really has to break through the clutter. From an advertising agency and creative perspective, we must understand and empathize with how a client comes up with a budget. There has to be a return on their investment in the marketing and sales arenas. Sometimes we at the agencies run off too arrogantly and say, "This is great advertising, so produce it," without understanding the repercussions nor the client companies' cash flow requirements.

You can measure return on investment in a myriad of ways. It has to be trackable, accountable, and make a profit. Whatever the costs of an advertising campaign, you start with what your client's expected returns or results are, then match the results in the marketplace from manufacturing to sales to distribution to product results, against those expectations.

Everything within a company has to work together, but I don't know many companies that can be successful for any length of time without having great marketing and great advertising to go with that great sales and distribution force behind it. I do believe that marketing, sales, and advertising are the soul of the economy.

Industry Insider

One of the biggest effects of technology is that it has stopped me from saying, "Don't worry, the layout is in the mail or with FedEx." Now I just send the PDF with a few clicks of a button. But more than that, the effects of technology have made us more aware, offering more choices and a confusing array of decision paths. They've sped up the communications. They've sped up the ability to gather information, to download, and to synthesize the situation. They've sped up the ability to know what's going on in France, Venezuela, and Iowa all at the same time and see the things that are similar and different. You can no longer claim that you can't know what's going on at a moment's notice. Speed has become a true discriminator in the marketplace.

Over the next three to five years, the large holding companies will start to shed assets. They've been terrific in terms of bringing a wide variety of experiences to the so-called "same page," but they have not always been structured for the client's benefit. Let's face it, they're for the benefit of their shareholders. As a craft, advertising must return to the essence of creating great communications and memorable moments. I do not believe that the holding company environment fosters this type of behavior: Creative and design boutiques, smaller, more facile organizations that punish bureaucracy will be the next winners.

Over time, I also think you'll see longer spots and a more continuous communication stream. With broadband, a 30-second spot can drive you into longer communication if you want it to. You may be giving permission to the brand to communicate with you in a more interactive, personal fashion with product line. With TiVo and others you can stop, go back, analyze – get the information in your time. The consumer is in charge. We have to explore different messaging lengths and systems, as well as streaming in different ways than today.

Technology will continue to change the way we do things. The globalization of the brand has been both good and bad. The essence of being able to go to Sweden, Sao Paulo, or San Francisco and buy different products based upon the local craftsman doesn't exist in that pure form anymore. We have to take that global thought and break it down to the charm of the nationality it belongs in. I have no idea where technology is actually going to take us but we must be prepared to grasp and love change. Flexibility will be paramount for success in the advertising world. Considering the speed with which we are being asked to create, I hope we don't lose the thought that real, original creativity, takes

time. Michelangelo would have had a tough time doing that
ceiling in two and a half days.

*G. Steven Dapper has spent his entire career in marketing
services. He began his direct marketing career at
Wunderman ("WCJ" a subsidiary of Young & Rubicam),
where he served as president of WCJ New York before being
named president & CEO of WCJ's North American
Operations in 1985 then Worldwide CEO in 1988. Dapper
built WCJ into the No. 1 direct response agency.*

*In 1991, he became CEO of Rapp Collins Worldwide, which
he built from the No. 6 direct response agency to No. 1,
surpassing WCJ. It had 31 offices from Sao Paulo to Dallas
to Paris and over 3,000 employees with accounts such as
Hyatt, Hilton, Continental Airlines, MCI and the U.S. Navy*

*Dapper created his present company, Hawkeye
Communications, in January 1999. It has grown from
Dapper and his Golden Retriever, Jessie, sitting above his
garage to an organization with over 500 employees in 10
offices in the U.S. and U.K.*

*Dapper sits on the board of directors of the Direct
Marketing Association (DMA). Steve is also on the Dean's
Advisory Board at Iowa State and NYU's Advisory Board for
Center for Direct and Interactive Marketing..*

Developing a Strategic Platform:
You Can't Just Wing It

David Hadeler
MARC USA, Dallas
President & CEO

Art, Science or Discipline?

Advertising is exclusively neither an art nor a science. It is part art, part science, and perhaps even a greater measure of discipline. If you don't have a disciplined approach to developing a strategic platform, it will be impossible to produce quality material over a long period of time.

The essential tactics for this type of disciplined approach are many: Hiring, training, firing, strategy development, creative development, media development, account service, research; how you follow up with your clients on a day to day basis; the processes you use within your agency; the financial discipline you have within your company; how you approach developing a real partnership with the client; how you approach developing an understanding of their products or services. So, discipline isn't something that's nice if you have time for it; it's mandatory. You can't just wing it.

In years past, advertising agencies have had the reputations of being free-thinking, free-wheeling, free-spending bastions of creative largesse where folks think, do and create great things all day long. But anyone who has worked in the business knows that the creative part is the figurative tip of the iceberg: It only represents about 10% of what we do. The rest of the time is spent learning, researching, understanding, and massaging information so that we can actually deliver a message that makes sense and produces results.

The Only Real Measurement – Results

Agencies and clients have tried forever to measure what
constitutes a successful campaign and have tried in many
different ways. They are still doing it today. Some attempt to
measure success by the recognition they receive, some by
rewards, others by client satisfaction.

In reality, though, the only real measure is in results. We are
hired to achieve results for our clients. Results can be
measured in different ways – market share, sales, or recall.
Without this type of measurement, how could you possibly
determine success? Still, work is produced every day that
isn't measured, and the opportunity to make that work better
by meaningful measurement goes by the wayside.

A common question is: How do you produce the best results?
There is no single best answer, because situations are unique
and demand unique solutions, but there are some tried and
true practices that can help you build a platform of service for
any client. You'll be able to respond to almost any marketing
challenge by establishing the client's brand, defending it,
delivering the message effectively, then staying flexible
enough to change and grow as circumstances dictate.

Clients Always Get the Advertising They Deserve

Numerous books have been and are being written every day
about branding. How to build brands, deliver them, and

support them successfully. For a brand to be truly established, it must be something that can deliver on its promise to its customers. To bring a brand to life, an agency must understand the client, its company, products or services, and its customers' past, present, and futures. The agency must also have a strong relationship with its client. There's an old agency saying that "clients usually get the advertising they deserve," meaning that clients with a solid long-term view will generally get better advertising than the client that insists on short-term results without building a solid foundation. Any agency veteran will tell you this is true.

A defined, long-term approach is vital. It is important to find a brand position then defend it position vigorously. If you have a defined position, your customers will seek you out and be loyal to you if they agree with that position. You are not going to be the answer for everyone or appeal to everyone, no matter what your product or service is. Companies that try to do this get frustrated and fail. Therefore, you have to find a position that is appropriate for you, your product, your service, your beliefs, and, most importantly, what you can deliver. Then you must build that position and defend it vigorously to deliver a consistent, effective message.

In its simplest form, advertising is a paid message. Compare it to public relations: PR is getting someone else to say something good about you, although you can't control when or where − or if − they will actually do it. Advertising is saying exactly what you want to say to the audience you

want, when and how often you want to say it. The only
downside is that you have to pay for it!

In the end, advertising isn't so much creating a brand or
position, or even selling a message. Typically, it depends
more on uncovering or discovering the message that exists
within the company, its product or what it can live up to. In
terms of creating a brand that people will remember, the key
word is "memorable." That is why so many of the best ads are
ones that touch you, either in a humorous way or in a
poignant way, but they really make you feel something, and
make you remember it.

Have a Message – Deliver it – Be Consistent

Over the life of any campaign or strategic push, there should
be one underlying theme. Although many messages can
weave in and out of that theme and support it, in any one
communication, it is easier and more beneficial to deliver one
important thought. If you think about the way companies
communicate today, they rarely rely on one way of
disseminating a message. Perhaps more important is that all
of the means of communication speak with one voice. If your
company brochure says one thing, your quarterly report says
another, your latest television commercial says another, your
Web site says something else, and then your company's CEO
is saying something completely different, you have a serious
issue. One of the most valuable services any agency can
provide to a client is to make sure the company is speaking

with one voice across all these platforms. This goes by many names – communications audit, message audit – but it is designed to make sure you are saying the same thing to all your constituents.

Sometimes people outside the industry think ad agencies simply create messages, positions or clever pictures for clients or companies. If you only create a message or a position for a company, and they are not equipped or willing to live up to it, then you are doing more harm than good. It would be harmful to create something they can't live up to. The ideal is to help them discover what and who they are, then sell that to the world in the best possible way.

Can brands survive forever? They can't without nurturing and evolving. People change. They get older. Tastes change. Needs change. At some point, the brand might need to reinvent itself. As a brand company or an agency that has the responsibility of shepherding a brand for the client, you have to stay aware of the changing competitive environment. If you are working for a client, it is your responsibility to help the client stay on top of this need.

Go Looking for Trouble

The one thing we absolutely know for sure is that things are going to change – customers, competition, the competitive environment, the economy, the world, and technology. If you're an advertising agency working with a client, or if you are a client professional responsible for marketing your company's product or service, you have to be ready to change in an instant to respond to any of these competitive challenges. If you want to be the best kind of leader, you also have to be prepared to seek out the things you need to change – you have to go looking for bad news. The client companies that are better, stronger, and more vibrant invariably have CEOs willing to go out and look for bad news and for things that need changing about their brand or company. They are willing to address customer needs, trends, and new directions, and they are not afraid to make a decision to do so.

If you just simply try to change your position to fit your customer base of the moment or try to change as your customers grow and evolve and die, your brand is going to grow and die with your customer base. In addition to nurturing and maintaining the established customer base, you must grow and attract new customers. It is all about evolving, changing and being willing to change with the world. I think this has become harder in recent times. Things are much more complex now than they were just a few years ago. And of course, a few years ago, we were saying that they were much more complex than they were a few years before that. Clients have changed. Client companies have changed. The entire operating environment of the agency world has changed. The world has also changed economically and politically. Everything is different.

The Changing Agency-Client Relationship

The client-agency relationship is different than it used to be. Clients expect and want agencies to deliver services differently, and agencies are working with clients in a very different manner from years ago.

One of the most significant changes between agencies and clients is in the relationship itself. Twenty years ago, agencies were more trusted advisors to client companies. They were held in the same esteem as other professional advisors, CPAs, attorneys, financial advisors. Over the years, for reasons not entirely clear, that relationship has changed. Generally speaking, relationships of today aren't as strong as they used to be. On the client side, for example, 20 to 25 years ago the typical client contact was older. They had been with the company for 12 to 15 years in a senior position. They anticipated being there another 12 to 15 years. They were interested in a long-term, consultative relationship, based on advice, trust, and knowledge. Today, client contacts have often been in the company for a much shorter period of time, perhaps only a few months. They don't anticipate being there much longer before they move on to the next world to conquer. When you have someone who has recently joined a company, the real impact that person can make is often by delivering something faster or cheaper. The relationship with the agency becomes more of a vendor-based relationship where they are asking you to deliver something faster or cheaper and not always better.

This unfortunately has strained the relationship between many agencies and clients and has been the cause of a less beneficial relationship between the two.

This has been very difficult on our industry. Our industry has been forced to find ways to do things much more quickly, much more cheaply, and that does not always mean doing them better. That has caused us to sometimes focus on hiring people based on how little we can pay them rather than how much they can benefit the company or the client. When you have to hire someone based on how fast and cheaply he will work, rather than on how much knowledge he brings to the client, you are rarely going to get as good a product or service for that client.

Future Relationships

The stronger agency-client relationships – if they are not already there – will move back toward a consultative relationship. For the most part, people who work in advertising agencies are extremely service-oriented, inquisitive to a high degree, and readily absorb knowledge in a number of disciplines (otherwise, they probably wouldn't be in this business). They have a good foundation in strategy and in all of the major disciplines – creative, account service, media and research. They are capable of providing sound, strategic advice and following through with all the elements to make those strategic foundations come true. The best agency/client relationships happen when the client allows its agency personnel to use this foundation of knowledge and skills.

The best thing that could happen for the advertising industry – and for most clients – would be to created an environment where agencies are valued more for the quality of the advice and work they deliver, rather than for how fast or how cheaply they can deliver it.

Risks vs. Risks

Fortunately, risk is usually not a life-or-death matter in advertising. That's not to say advertising decisions aren't important. Indeed, some advertising decisions are critically important and can mean – literally – whether a company stays in business or not. Sometimes those decisions are based on a lot of information, and sometimes decisions are based on very little or no information. Sometimes the most important decision is to decide not to do anything at all for a client. We always try to advise the client as if we were advising ourselves.

One of the issues in our industry is that we are not licensed the way CPAs or attorneys are. As an industry, we routinely hand out advice involving client budgets of millions of dollars, and clients routinely take that advice. Almost anyone can hang out an advertising or marketing shingle, but unfortunately not all of them know what they are doing. It is entirely possible that a company could be put out of business by accepting bad advice about a budget, position, direction, or message. Most advertising professionals take the responsibility of helping companies very seriously by giving them sound strategic advice.

How Do You Keep Up?

There is not enough time in the day to keep up on all of the industry knowledge. In a collaborative business like advertising, it is important to stay involved, grow, learn about the client business, stay aware of competitive factors, and share that knowledge. This is a responsibility of not only the agency but the client partner as well. If you are not willing to share information, it is not an effective partnership. In today's highly competitive atmosphere, you must have everyone rowing in the same direction. Clients must share information, agencies must share information, and everyone must discuss that information and work together. Of course, it is impossible as one company, one agency, or one person to stay as informed as you need to be. There is too much information. Still, you have to try.

Pitfalls

Not all clients understand what an advertising agency is and what an agency can do for them. Clients sometimes use the terms advertising, marketing, PR, branding, positioning and design interchangeably (and sometimes incorrectly).

From a client perspective, it is important to hire an agency that is a good fit for you and your company. It is important that the agency be given the opportunity to understand what you are doing – your business, your competitors, your goals, your needs. Of course, it helps clients understand what their own needs are.

On the agency side, agencies must be careful about the companies or clients they choose. As agencies, we are what we eat when it comes to our client list. If you take on bad clients, you are going to do bad work for them and for the agency.

There is an old saying in the industry I've heard agency veterans repeat over the years. There are two variations of it. One variation says that good clients get good advertising. The other less kind variation is that clients get the advertising they deserve. That is true. Great clients, if they deserve great advertising, will get great advertising. They don't just invest money. They invest knowledge, time, information, a willingness to work as a partner, and an adequate budget to make it happen. If a client is looking for a quick fix, doesn't want to share information, won't take the time to meet and discuss, and doesn't want to take the initiative to fund it, they will most assuredly not get what they expect from their agency relationship.

Unfortunately, agencies are put all too often in the position of having to create the proverbial silk purse out of a sow's ear, especially when they are ill-informed and poorly budgeted.

This is a set up for failure. Ad agencies continue to take on work because they are service-oriented; it is a highly competitive industry now and everyone takes on almost every account that walks in front of them. It's a very risky business to be in these days.

Risk or not, we still fight over every client and every prospect. We still do it because we get highly charged by the thrill of the chase. We want to do great things for clients. We want to help them succeed. We love the challenge of developing the strategy. We love the challenge of matching that strategy with the right creative.

The Value of Service

The best piece of advertising advice I ever received was from a former boss who said to always make sure you give more value than the client anticipates, and that you provide more value than the client has paid for. What this is telling us is: Don't leave anything on the table. Don't do a half-hearted effort.

That advice includes the practice of hiring. The old adage about the weakest link couldn't be more true than in the advertising business. Over the years I have tried to hire folks who know a lot more than I do in every discipline. Fortunately, that hasn't been too difficult. I have managed to hire some absolutely incredible talent, and I have encouraged

them to hire incredible talent. I have managed to run some
very good companies as a result.

Talent isn't enough, though. A strong service ethic is vital. If
you don't have a strong service ethic, and you are not willing
to work to take the extra step to do the job better than it could
or should be done, then advertising is going to be a tough
business for you to work in. It is very important, particularly
for a young person getting into the industry today, to realize
that this is a service business. Granted, it is a business of
products, creative and strategy, but the overriding element
that ties these together – especially in long-tenured
relationships – is service. It is a service business.

Although the world in which advertisers and their agencies
are operating is getting more complex every day, success can
still be achieved. I believe it is possible to outwork the other
guys rather than just outspending them. I believe that what we
do in advertising is special and that not everyone can do it. I
believe that a great agency promotes the client and the brand,
and not the agency. Bottom line, though, the work agencies
do isn't all that creative if it doesn't achieve results.

Above all, I believe in the old-fashioned concept of
partnership. I believe in helping clients grow. I believe it is
important to hire young, bright people, to nurture and train
them, and to help them believe that every project they do for
any client is the most important project they will ever handle.
I believe in accountability. I believe in results. And, I believe

that you can do all of this and still have a lot of fun in the business.

David Hadeler is the president and CEO of the Dallas office of MARC USA, the fourth largest independent advertising and marketing services firm in the United States. In addition to helping build some of the best-known brands in the country, he has participated in the launch of new products, in the positioning and repositioning of national brands, and has helped develop advertising and marketing campaigns for everything from fishing reels to airlines, and from fast food to foreign imports.

A graduate of Baylor University, he received his graduate degree from The University of North Texas, where he is an advisory board member of the School of Communications. He is involved in a number of civic activities, and serves on the boards of several national charitable organizations.

Company to Customer Relationship: The Business of Building Businesses

Paul S. Allen

Allen & Gerritsen

CEO

Succeeding in the Advertising World

Success in advertising requires the ability to have a fundamental grasp of both sides of our business. First is the strategic side, providing marketing counsel and tactical marketing help for our clients' businesses. To communicate and advertise effectively on behalf of a business, you need to look at a client's company and conceptualize it. This means not just looking at the hard products and services it sells and what benefits they bring to customers, but understanding theoretically what that client's business is all about: having a deep understanding of the business's fundamental disciplines and being able to analyze it objectively. The other side involves creativity and communication: the ability to take that conceptual understanding and turn it into communications, messages, and advertising truly connected to the strategy.

Advertising is not simply an art, it is a science and an art, and I believe the science is getting more important. Science will make the art do necessary things: create action and make the delivery more appropriate. More and more, it is less about how you say something (the creative) and more about what you're actually saying. Messages must be more meaningful and relevant to the target audiences to earn their notice and acceptance. Companies must try to fit into their customers' lives versus just talking at them. The science of strategic messaging is what adds the insights and new perspectives that drive communications.

At the end of the day, our business runs into the same commoditization problems that affect any industry. We all think about creative then we make creative. Our differentiation—or at least the thing we have really focused on—is our proprietary models on the strategic side of the equation. We are trying to change the way clients think about relationships with their customers and the way they think about how they need to articulate it. We fundamentally believe that the disciplines of positioning and branding have gotten stale and that agencies need to provide a better level of competitive advantage to their clients—and that first occurs when you think about the strategic side of the business. We believe the way to make effective, creative advertising is to revisit how you think about it in terms of the company-to-customer relationship.

The opportunity that we have uncovered—and it is the root of our practice—is not to think about the company's positioning, branding and all the messages we need to bring to market, but to help clients think determine their fundamental role with their customers. We have hit upon a role-based model that gets companies and clients thinking less about their advertising and what to say than about who they really are and how they earn a right to have an ongoing role in their customers' lives. There is a very different method to our madness here.

In today's economy, our markets lack value and earnings; I think this is also true in the agency environment. History has shown that earnings and value come not by innovating but by sustained innovation. The advertising industry is long overdue for sustained innovation.

Excitement and Challenges

I started this business almost 20 years ago because I felt our industry—which is exciting and a great way to make a living—could be more fundamentally important to our clients' businesses. I left other agencies and created my own because I felt advertising and communications could make a stronger contribution than they have. I personally enjoy a business that combines the challenges of strategic and creative thinking, and this business is unique since you must be able to link the two ways of thinking. Finally, it's interesting to have only people and their minds as the assets that help build businesses. We do not have plants and equipment. We do not have giant factories. What we do have is a community of people and their talents, their goodwill and their intelligence. Having a talented group focused on helping businesses with tangible goods to sell is an incredible experience, for us as an agency and for our client partners. This is a fascinating business, and there is a lot of opportunity to make it more important with clients and with marketers.

The exciting part, and part of our enormous responsibility, is manifesting what a company tries to say, do, or be. While a lot of people look at our business as show business—we do television commercials and are perceived to be all about creativity—our real responsibility is to translate a business, promotion, or offer and make it publicly visible. It is an exciting thing to do but also requires responsibility because a business plan is a business plan and a strategy is a strategy, but until it becomes visible and creative nobody knows about it. We make visible that to which a company aspires, in the most visible of ways.

One of the challenges is trying to help a company get focused and energized about what they are offering. Often clients and companies are not in entire agreement internally about who they are, what they should be, and what they should say. We work very hard on behalf of our clients to make sure they are focused and unified. I think that is a big obligation for agencies and a major pitfall if it does not happen.

There is always the other challenge of investing a client's money properly. We are given lots of room to spend and invest. A big challenge is how to best spend and invest on behalf of a client's business and brand. By investing in only what's important (what makes sense for the target audience and what will build the brand and drive sales concurrently), an agency can truly help grow its client's business.

Finally, we have a social responsibility. We are operating in an environment of incredible economic and social change. The context in which people receive images and messages about companies, clients, and marketers today is dramatically different than it was only a few decades ago. Our industry really needs to be socially conscious as we make our clients visible.

We also need to stay abreast of the changes that are going on in the advertising world, in our client's businesses, and in the business world at-large. What do you do to stay on top of your advertising knowledge? You check in with several different worlds. The first is the client world: you can never lose touch with what real clients are dealing with every day. You learn a lot just from your client immersion and understanding in real time what is going on. We subscribe to all sorts of information services and get real-time perspectives on our clients, their categories, and business at-large. A number of outside consulting firms keep us abreast of what is going on in a given industry. I am fortunate to be involved in several forums and think tanks where I am with people who are also thinking about what is next. Staying immersed and educated in as many dimensions as we can and using that to fuel our idea of how we help our clients is vital.

Establishing a Brand

You cannot build a brand with advertising alone. Advertising is only one connection with the customer. We don't believe branding is a set of activities: branding is an outcome. You do not have a brand by hoping to have a brand. You have a brand by doing a lot of things that meet your aspiration. One recent fallacy was the notion you could build a brand by doing "branding things." Instead, if you advertise, communicate, behave differently, do things, and say things, the net result will be that you will have a brand. In fact, if you don't do anything you have a brand. The question is how much of your brand do you want to control?

Building a brand (not to minimize what we do, because it is very important) involves everything from a company's fundamental proposition to a customer's experience going into a store. Building an established brand is not just a communication activity: It is all the activities that converge on a customer. For example, you may see a great piece of advertising for XYZ stores and love the way the brand looks, and you may like the price and the promotion, but you walk into that store and the person behind the counter says three things that annoy you. That one person has completely changed your impression of that brand. The airlines are a great example of this. You can promote the image of the "friendly skies" or service, but it only takes one surly flight attendant to ruin the brand for customers. Building an established brand involves not only making a promise, but also making good on that promise through a consistent experience.

A brand cannot survive by staying in one place. Brands must evolve: react to markets and environments as they change; understand evolving customers; stay involved in what is going on within the company. A brand can survive a long time. Look at Coca-Cola, Johnson & Johnson, and General Electric. Brands like those and IBM (a completely different company than it was 20 years ago but still a robust, contemporary brand) don't survive by accident. They survive by paying close attention to all the changes. Brands can survive a long time, but not by standing still.

A Successful Advertising Campaign

From an advertising standpoint it has gotten more complicated to keep brands fresh. If you had a product when television transitioned from black-and-white to color, that changed a lot of things, too. But with today's technology, the information age, the dissolving of borders, and a global marketplace, it is more complicated to maintain a brand.

Twenty years ago you could reach 80 percent of a certain demographic with one television buy. Now you have to buy 20 different channels to do that. There are exponentially more pieces of information from which to net out simple, compelling, motivating, creative advertisements. It is infinitely more complex and fragmented.

At its simplest, a successful advertising campaign helps move a client's business goals forward. We do not advertise for entertainment or for the sake of producing great creative. Our point of view states that if you invest in advertising it must move your business somewhere. The movement can be from simply making a larger segment of the right people more aware of your offering to actually getting people into stores or increasing sales. If it does not create some sort of desired action then it is a failure. There are a wide range of actions that advertising and communications can instigate. At its simplest, advertising must do something or don't bother investing in it.

A company or a product must have an overarching value proposition or a fundamental premise to offer a market. The greatest opportunity lies, however, in using the various communication channels — advertising, Internet, direct marketing, event marketing—to send the components of that proposition out to the market in different forms factors. For example, with one large retail client, an overarching brand proposition is used in the widest medium, television, but many important sub-messages go into a promotion or price offers at a store event that aren't communicated though advertising. Today it is about multiple messages through multiple channels, but they all have to subscribe to a fundamental value proposition from the client.

A campaign should accurately reflect in a creative way who the company is, the product or the service being communicated. It cannot be an over-promise; it cannot be conjecture or fabricated. It has to be—creatively—a real picture of who the advertiser is. For us there are three principles that go behind the question, "When is advertising both effective and truthful?" One, the act of advertising must add value to those who are receiving it, e.g., a television commercial runs and someone either learns something or was genuinely entertained. The rule is: Don't communicate and don't advertise if the act of it doesn't add some value. We also have an obligation to create a clear opportunity for those who are receiving it. Finally, there's the concept of mutual respect: All of our creative portrayal must seriously respect those to whom we are speaking. In terms of creative, it must reflect the company's aspiration, but then don't waste people's time and money unless you are going to put something fairly meaningful, albeit creative, in front of them.

Avoiding Pitfalls

One pitfall for advertisers to avoid is talking about internal issues outside the company. An enormous number of companies want to talk about and advertise things that are irrelevant to outside audiences but big topics of discussion inside a company. For example, a client may want to advertise that it has this division and that division. Customers don't care.

Second, many companies invest in the basics, spending a lot of money on stuff that is a basic premise of their business. For example, an Internet security company wants to tell the market it is in the security business. No kidding. Research shows that the market did not want to hear the company is in the security business; it already knew that. The market wanted to hear that by using these security services it could do things with IT systems it couldn't do before. A lot of times advertisers say things that are obvious: what everyone expects them to say. It would be like the Boston Bruins doing an ad that says, "We play hockey."

Third, avoid treating advertising like show business. A ludicrous amount of money is spent in the production and creation of materials. What clients spend on interesting techniques and devices borders on the irresponsible when you are using a company's money to promote capitalist things with consumers.

And finally, always be cognizant of the language or lexicon used in messaging. Many companies use internal jargon and acronyms that mean nothing to potential customers, creating instant barriers to acceptance of their messages. It's a basic premise: If they don't know what you're talking about, chances are they're not going to buy it.

Budgeting

Many factors go into budgeting. Some companies do fundamental work on a percentage of sales, and there are standards for various industries and categories. Advertising should be X percent of sales, and then we make the most of that X percent of sales.

A lot of it also depends on the goal. If we want to change minds, we will undoubtedly spend more at that point in time because we are trying to offset perceptions that already exist.

Additionally, spending is sometimes reliant on the business model of the client company. Some companies sell one thing, they can put all their money behind one thing, and then they sell that one thing. That requires a different level of investment than a company that has seven divisions and seven product lines that all go to different channels and different customers. That type of company is going to have to spend more because there is a lot more going on.

Finally, a lot of it is determined by who the customer is and what the quantified population is. Ultimately, if there are seven million people in the country who might buy your product, you have to figure out how to talk to them—and there are certain costs associated with that.

A number of factors affect budgeting. It can be as simple as a percentage of sales, but more often you take in audience population, client business model, and the ultimate cost of the various media. Advertising in Indianapolis is not as expensive as advertising in Boston. If there are stores in Boston and stores in Indianapolis, we might do different things in those markets, too.

And lastly, when budgeting, always take into account return on investment or ROI. There are many ways to measure it. There are two columns. One is qualitative, the other is quantitative. The qualitative usually leads to the quantitative. On the qualitative side, many means can measure if you have changed someone's perception. Has a larger group of people become more aware? Have we convinced people who were aware to be now predisposed? Have we caused people to get off their couches and go to our stores? Quite a number of qualitative methods and research methodologies can be used to understand whether we have changed someone's mind and influenced the way they think. On the quantitative side, it gets down to: Have we improved sales? Have we improved profitability? Have we opened new distribution channels? Have these 10 new stores met their sales goals once we opened them? It comes down to fact. There are two fields of measurement: qualitative (what did we make people think?) and quantitative (what did we make people do?).

Changes in the Advertising Industry

There has been a great deal of evolution in the advertising business. Some change has been driven from inside the industry; some has been driven by customers and clients. Our industry gets yanked, pulled, and morphed by whatever is happening around it. In the last five or 10 years we have seen some major shifts. On the strategic side of the business, we continue to see an evolution in the thinking behind advertising. Ten or 15 years ago it was all about the "unique selling proposition" that said one thing about a client or a product that would really get someone's attention to make them buy it. That has since evolved into the discipline of positioning, figuring out how to get a share of your competitive markets. That was enhanced by the discipline of branding, where companies were worried about their identity and their share of mind. We have seen first and foremost a real evolution in the thinking behind advertising. One of the things we are concerned about is taking that thinking to a new and more provocative level.

On the creative side, the evolution has really been in the channels through which messages are communicated. Ten years ago, we would talk only about advertising; today advertising is only one of all the various channels available to communicate. More than ever it is less about advertising than about how you create the most meaningful messages and how you send them out through advertising, direct marketing, Internet, and one-to-one sales engagements. On the creative side, the biggest challenge is how to use all the access points that are available, because it is no longer solely about advertising.

In the future, marketers, companies, and clients are going to scrutinize more carefully what they spend, what they say, and where they say it. Particularly with the rise and fall of the dot-com era, a lot of disciplines and ways agencies helped clients—and ways agencies believed brands could and should be built—were proven wrong. Frankly, I do not think our industry has reflected long and hard enough on how bad a job most advertising agencies did during that period of time.

In the future, all communications are going to have to earn their way into a customer's life. With the advent of TiVo and EchoStar, just because you created a television commercial does not mean anybody is going to want to see it. An overarching trend, then, is that just because you make it does not mean that anybody will want to hear it. Advertising is going to have to make the communication desirable. The 30-second spot could become obsolete. It will become harder to get it to somebody. If something is harder to get to somebody and harder to show them, that form factor will change. In the short term, we will continue to use the 30-second spot, but in the long term it could become obsolete.

We will also see a major backlash in content, particularly in the broadcast environment. Some research shows that reality television and violence—although compelling and interesting to the viewer—are terrible programs during which to remember advertising. They are also the most expensive segments on television. A backlash will occur when advertisers realize the most expensive places in broadcast media turn out to be terrible places to run commercials because viewers are not taking in the messages.

Finally, people are going to look at communications now more than ever and assume it reflects the leaders, the company CEOs. We are not doing commercials on behalf of some retail chain; we are doing them on behalf of that retail chain's CEO. The reflection of corporate leadership in communications should get a lot of consideration moving forward.

Golden Rules and Advice

There are three key rules for successful advertising. First, good advertising should be self-evident. Agencies should not have to "sell" their campaigns to their clients. When an agency does its job on behalf of a client, the client says, "You have helped us find ourselves. Now let's go to market with that."

Second, have respect for the audience. While we are here to entertain and engage, we are foremost here to be respectful of the people whose time we are taking and to whom we are trying to sell something.

Third, bring it back to business. We are in an industry that should help build the businesses of our clients. We are fortunate to be in a fun industry, but it is still about business. It is time that our industry brought it back to business. Beyond marketing and communications, we are in the business of building businesses.

One final piece of advice: Think about something but don't over think it. If you feel in your gut that something is the right thing to do, don't over think it. You are going to waste time. If you really believe something is right, do it. For all the good thinking in our world and all the good research, at some point you have to have enough experience under your belt, enough conviction and enough knowledge to just make a decision to do something and do it well.

After a successful career in several of the region's most well-known agencies, including BBDO and Ingalls, Paul Allen followed his entrepreneurial instincts and founded Allen & Gerritsen. As CEO, he is responsible for the overall management of the $150+ million shop and strategic vision of the business.

Over a decade ago, Allen recognized the value of partnering with clients in high performance industries. His vision gave birth to A&G's proprietary practice that redefines companies' relationships with their customers to the greatest advantage. A&G's success is based on combining this proprietary strategic practice with a nationally recognized creative product.

Allen is a recognized industry innovator. He has published a series of articles in publications such as Knowledge Management, B2B, The Business to Business Marketer, DM News, The Advertiser, and Marketing Computers.

Allen is chairman of long-range strategic planning for the Boston Ad Club.

He grew up in Norwood, MA, and has a degree in economics from Lafayette College. When he's not traveling around the world for agency clients, he sails his boat "Pinneped" around the coast of Maine.

Beyond Traditional Boundaries: Being Creative & Inventive

Joe Grimaldi

Mullen Advertising

President & CEO

The Art and Science of Advertising

Advertising has been described as something that interrupts someone's attention long enough to be able to sell them something.   Fundamentally, you're imposing yourself – intruding upon someone's time and finding a way to connect with a passive mind in a very brief period to help inform or intrigue with something that has value to that person. That's what advertising is. The art relates to the entertainment qualities, which are there to capture interest. The science is in the ability to understand what you're going to do when you have those two or three seconds of attention. The science involves having an understanding of people and human nature; understanding the qualities of a product, a brand, a category, or a specific offering and being able to frame it properly.

Building Brands, Maintaining Relevance

The best definition of a brand is all of the thoughts, feelings, and associations that come to mind when you're exposed to the logo, symbol or anything else that triggers a particular branded image. The first thing that makes a brand strong is a passionate love for it. In building brands, we take a product or service and try to position it so that someone falls in love with it, and that love turns it into a brand. It takes it out of a commodity buy and turns it into something that is very close and dear to me and that I value.

Established brands have several characteristics. First, they have recognition and awareness: That's critical. Second, they are relevant to the consumer in some deep way. That's where the passion and love really come from. The third critical factor is that the brand or product experience (the packaging, delivery and support systems) reinforces everything you believe in a way that makes it strong. A brand is something that emerges on the scene and captures your passion. Every time you engage in it or deal with it creates an experience that not only delivers on a promise that was offered, but actually enhances you in some way.

There are probably a lot of old, established brands – a couple that come immediately to mind are Tide or Heinz Ketchup – that can survive forever. The question is: What kills an established brand, or why does a brand not survive? The answer: when a brand loses its relevance to its target customers. Take Tide as an example. If I recall correctly, Tide was the first powder detergent that ever hit the market. Today, if Tide were still saying, "We're the powder detergent," it wouldn't be in business. Today, Tide is talking about being either the brightest or the whitest or providing color in cold water – whatever it is. What they did all along, though, was evolve the product to be relevant to a consumer's lifestyle, and they evolved the communications to be relevant to that consumer's lifestyle. The brand is something you're aware of, something deeply and emotionally relevant to you beyond its rational factors, something that creates an experience that delivers on a promise and maybe even adds to you in some way. That's what it really takes.

There are many examples of brands that became irrelevant. The technology business is one area where this has happened. Take a look at Digital Equipment Corporation: It was one of the largest companies out there. Or Prime. These companies were built around the concept of mini-computers. Whatever happened to mini-computers? Nobody uses them anymore. They became preempted by other things. In the automotive industry, you have brands that have been out there for a long time. Mercedes-Benz and Ford have been around for a long time as brands. Again, it's been due to meeting the consumer's needs, anticipating and delivering something that meets those consumer needs, and communicating about it in an effective way. The brands that die are the brands that fail to recognize that consumers are changing, the world is changing, needs are changing, the way we do things is changing, the way we absorb things is changing. But it doesn't have to be that way if you're vigilant and keep changing yourself.

Consistent Messages

First and foremost, you want to define your brand or your positioning in very fundamental ways. Whatever drives that brand – the governing brand idea – should be consistent throughout your communications. That consistency should not deviate, otherwise you run the risk of confusing consumers. You need to stand for something. If you're a cause, the cause should clearly be understood. If you're an enabler, what you enable should be clearly understood. If you're a statement of who I am or what I am, that statement should be clearly understood. I think, however, that you can make judgments about how to express that in order to be relevant to the people you want to express it to.

A general rule when launching something new is to keep for some period of time not only the governing brand idea, positioning or fundamental proposition the same, but also to keep the executions relatively consistent. The reason is to maximize establishing the core idea. The more I can repeat it and build frequency, the better off I am. As brands become more established, you want to do more than just execute. You want to think about how the consumer is going to engage with that particular execution through a particular avenue. If you're doing guerrilla postings, your execution might involve a more fun approach, which might be different than a television approach. For example, if you are talking about a social product such as beer, the execution might take on a slightly different flavor in that kind of environment. But you want the positioning to be consistent.

Take the example of Sony. Sony stands for something. To most people, Sony stands for the absolute ultimate in consumer electronics products. It's the highest quality performance product. However, if you look across the set of executions Sony might do, which are done by a variety of agencies, the actual executions might be a little different if you're talking to someone buying Sony Playstation 2 versus someone buying a Sony Vega plasma TV screen. One costs $200, the other costs $17,000, and they're purchased for different reasons. The general rule is you want the core positioning in a brand idea to be alive and well in everything. Also, you want to drive for a core idea that is relevant and utilizes the media. It is important that the consumer engages it in a way that maximizes that opportunity.

Maximizing a Budget

Advertising tactics vary based on budget. In an ideal world, the level of innovation brought to a small budget should be brought to a large budget as well. You should constantly strive for fresh, different ideas on how to maximize the return on that dollar.

You can go in and determine an advertising-to-sales ratio, and some categories are naturally higher than others. Retail has a fairly high advertising-to-sales ratio because it's demand-driven. You might have categories where it's 3 percent, and others where it's 15 percent. There are rules of thumb that say how much you should be spending. The reality is that spending is enabled by the amount of money available, but the logic that drives spending should always maximize the returns. If you're dealing with a smaller budget, usually you're trying to find ways to zig when everyone else is zagging. You've got to find other ways to engage a consumer's attention and have them connect with it. If you can afford the Super Bowl, that's pretty cool too, but you need to find inventive ways of doing it. Case in point: Several years ago Victoria's Secret did a runway show, an advertising piece, that later went to the web. It was really interesting and extremely well-viewed. That was a very inventive use of high-cost advertising. The agency's job is to maximize return on investment no matter what the number is. There might be times when an agency should advise its client to take a radically different view, because it cannot compete in traditional ways based on the amount of money available. That is not unusual. For example, a certain cleaning product started out with heavy-duty infomercial demonstrations that built the business by buying relatively low-rated TV airtime when the time was cheap. A man would demonstrate the product, and people would buy direct. Then the company went to traditional advertising, not an infomercial but more of a direct-response commercial. Now you can go to a retail channel and buy that product. Here is a company that probably did not have the resources to compete against the traditional detergent and bleaching products: to get all the distribution, run $25-35 million worth of advertising against "homemakers" and build the business that way. It came out in a fresh, radical way. I don't know how big the business is now, but it has to be a reasonable size because it has the retail distribution and is running more traditional kinds of advertising. Coming at it in an entirely different way maximized the long-term return.

You have to look at advertising and media in totally different ways. You think about media as not being just paid media. You think about how to maximize visibility, how to maximize the impact of every dollar spent. You look at it in nontraditional ways – you're not just talking about traditional media. The lines between the media vehicles and what's advertising and what's not advertising start to blur dramatically. You don't know where the paid advertising stops and the non-paid advertising takes over. It takes on a very different texture. That maximizes the budget, but you've got to use a similar kind of thinking even if you're working with a big budget.

The other way to maximize a budget is by the inventiveness of your creative communication solutions. One of our current clients is a brand called LendingTree.com, an online loan marketplace. It came after e-Loan but has obliterated the competition in about three years, becoming the No. 1 brand in that business. We run a lot of television advertising (also radio and print) and measure the return on investment on every dollar we spend in a variety of ways. It looks like very traditional advertising, but the trick to that solution was really in the positioning. We harnessed the power of a latent emotion that consumers had and turned it into something positive. Consumers think banks abuse them. We turned the tables on the power and put the consumer in control of the bank. That's just a very strong emotional drive. A creative solution can maximize the return on a budget, so even though we may not spend as much as other people do, we get a lot more back for the money.

Successful Advertising: The Obvious and Not-So-Obvious

For advertising to be successful, you must have a product or service that will fulfill the promise of the advertising campaign. Otherwise, it's a bad idea. First, a successful ad campaign is an idea rooted in a potent, powerful consumer insight. It is something that a consumer, while engaging with the message or proposition, feels "is part of me and I am part of it." He or she should use it or become part of the cause or use it to express part of who they are. Second, the expression of that advertising execution must be theatrical and really jar the consumers' interest and imagination. It must ask them to spend a few seconds with us, but they must opt into it on their own, and there is power behind that. Third, it must find a way to engage in a consumer's life at a time and point that is relevant. Fourth, it must continue to evolve in the same way the consumer is evolving, so it can continue to be cumulative.

It sounds quite simple, but that is basically what you need to do. If you want to take a financial perspective on how you create the impact potential, you must ensure that you have the ability as a total entity, a campaign, to break through the threshold of indifference and put a spear through the consumer's heart so he's enamored of something. As you think about a campaign in a more holistic way, you have to create a sequence of experiences or touch points with the consumer that brings them all the way from something they fall in love with to something they will buy to an experience that will make them want to buy again. That constitutes a successful advertising program.

To be successful, you also must avoid the major pitfalls: ideas that don't have merit; executions that are brilliant but no one remembers what they're for; promises that are so inconsistent with the actual product or service delivery that advertising becomes its biggest enemy because you've create unmet expectations. Those are all pretty obvious. A subtler element in a very complex market is to make sure a consumer understands that your brand is different. If you fail to do that, you become ordinary and fail to be differentiated. Distribution is another major failure point. You must figure in the distribution and the availability of a product in a relevant way. If you're running advertising to empty shelves, you may be making a mistake. If you have a certain amount of promotion within your advertising and communication plan, over-promoting a product when it first comes out can devalue it over the long term. Many small mistakes can be made, but the biggest ones relate to making a promise that will create disappointment, creating communications that are so wonderfully entertaining that they fail to sell something, or just making it so irrelevant to the consumer that it doesn't matter.

The best thing people in the advertising business can do is buy large stacks of magazines on a regular basis and look through them frequently. You have to be culturally attuned with the people you're trying to sell. One of the ways to do that is to absorb the culture and trends and what's going on. It's not just magazines, but also television programs.

Sometimes I watch television programs I normally wouldn't watch – like Road Rules, The Sopranos, or Six Feet Under – because those shows are important to people today and that's what they're watching. Those shows are social currency and a strong indication of how people are thinking about life and how they're finding their entertainment. It is critical that we stay contemporary. I often listen to my kids' music for the very same reasons. The notion of staying culturally attuned is critical. It's not just about marketing smarts, it's about marketing smarts in a relevant way. The relevancy is defined by the consumer's life.

Changes in the Industry

The advertising industry has changed in very radical ways. The industry has been repositioned because clients have problems that often require a broader set of tools or a broader set of consultants to help them solve. So, to some degree, advertising has been redefined by the Internet, by direct marketing, by public relations, by CRM, by management consultants. That has happened because client problems have become much more complex as a function of the world becoming much more complex.

Technology has had a major influence on that. Who would have thought 10 or 15 years ago that you would have an HTML programmer working inside your company – and not even in the technology group. Today they are part of a marketing group: part of an interactive group that is part of a brand team that works on a client's business. Those are radical changes. Companies such as Sapient, Agency.com and Modem Media have entered the scene, and these companies have had radical impact. During recent wild times, companies such as AOL and Time Warner brought their properties together; their interest was in going directly to clients and hitting clients with propositions. So there are many different things going on, with a variety of players trying to participate in what was, years ago, a different kind of agency role – the creative aspect of the business. Now you've got technology companies in the creative business. I think that's how the industry has changed, and it gave birth to a lot of different types of companies. It required agencies to learn how to buy interactive media. It created tracking systems for interactives and hits and many different things. It has also imploded to some degree. But like everything else, it didn't change back to what it was – it just evolved. In the process, the agencies lost many people to these other companies, then the industry contracted and lost a lot more people.

An interesting thing happened to our industry in the late '70s or early '80s, when the middle of the agency hierarchy – people like account supervisors, associate media directors and media supervisors – disappeared because the revenues weren't there to support them. These people were like sergeants in the military, the ones who knew everything and could teach new recruits in an aggressive, substantive way. They could also relate to senior management and provided a way for people coming into the business to learn it well. It lined them up to become future leaders – the ones who were good enough. When you take that layer out, the training is not as good and eventually the caliber of leadership is not very good. The truth is that there is a lack of very top-level, smart, capable leadership in our industry (as in many industries – I don't believe it's unique to the advertising business). That has happened because the brightest minds follow where the business goes. It used to be in advertising, then it went to other places, and eventually it ended up in investment banking and venture capital. Quite frankly, I don't know where it is right now, because it's still going around.

Beyond the industry, the advertising itself has changed. I'm not sure it's changed as radically as the industry has, but you can see how ads are starting to change. Advertising has actually changed because the nature of the environment has changed. Advertising used to be 30-second commercials, and every once in a while you'd hear of "guerrilla marketing" or "under-the-radar marketing," but that wasn't the norm. The palette of what you define as advertising or creativity – if the purpose is to create an encounter with a consumer to present a cause and ask them to join or to make a proposition to them – doesn't have to be done that way. Some of the very visible venues right now are the BMW films; online experiences designed to entertain people, bring them in and form relationships with them. Commercial products have always been integrated into movies. In 1985, we had the Puma business and when A Chorus Line was made we were putting product placements in there. Coke has been in there forever. But now people are looking for new, different ways to do that. You get concepts that start in a 30-second commercial then bleed onto online; that's just based on the fact that the consumer is changing. Here's an interesting statistic: about 45 percent of people with computers have them in the same room as their principal television set. I think about 80 percent are people watching television while on the computer. You've got a large number of people engaged in multi-media – the television as well as the computer. In many cases, these people are doing something related to the program. What you start to see is a dialogue that might start with one medium and move into another.

The way advertising is done is changing, and that's a reflection of how our world is changing. Advertising must engage the consumer. Consumers are changing – they absorb media differently, they see the world differently, and advertising has to reflect that. One thing frequently said is that the latest generations – Generation X, Generation Y, and so on – are population groups that understand advertising as a promotional vehicle. They don't like being sold to. Advertising has to serve a different role for them, so it's about creating engagements and encounters and, therefore, the media has to reflect it. That changes the way you use your advertising and what the content of your advertising message is.

Advertising is fundamentally a way to market, and that hasn't changed. The basic principle or driving philosophy behind advertising is still the same. What you're trying to do is figure out how to use communications – whether traditional communications on television or in print, or nontraditional communications which might be field marketing or engagements, for example – to do the same thing. So the fundamental role and objective of the game has not changed. The level of inventiveness and how you think about solving problems has changed and influenced the business.

The future changes of advertising will relate to two things. First, the consumer. What are consumers doing with their lives and how do they interact with the media? Let's say that things like TiVo really start to take hold (and I'm not sure they will, because there are a lot of infrastructure issues associated with that). When consumers are not watching commercials, who will pay for the program development for commercial TV? You have to figure out a way to outsmart consumer behavior. The way to outsmart that is to integrate advertising communications messages right within the programming itself, so you don't get that split-second break that notifies a device you're now going to a commercial break. The things that consumers believe in and think about and what they value will fundamentally change advertising. September 11 had an influence on the advertising business and will continue to have an influence not because of patriotism but because consumers stood back and said, "What's really important to me? Family is really important to me. Spending time is really important to me." That's had an impact on cultural movements – kitchens and great rooms are again the big thing because that's the heart of the house. Part of that has been accelerated by things like September 11th, terrorism and the prospect of war.

The second factor that will influence how advertising continues to change is technology and what it enables. When broadband really comes in and has availability beyond its current 15 to 18 percent, the possibilities of what you can do with that start to change radically.

Advertising and Company Vision

There was a time when advertising CEOs had very close relationships and personal, trusted, valued relationships with the CEOs of their clients. This was in the early days of advertising when advertising was an extremely powerful tool in the '50s and the '60s and even before that. It enabled clients to build their brands and their businesses in strong ways. The brand became a franchise mechanism. It was a new and powerful tool – television created a new and powerful tool. A relationship existed at that level and has evolved over time.

As new tools came about, and as new types of problems and complexities occurred, clients broadened their views of what kinds of solutions they needed; I think agencies might have gotten a little bit stuck on just advertising solutions. CEOs of client companies brought in more people, and the relationship that was very unique and special between the senior management of a client organization and an advertising agency was not as revered anymore. There were other people in the mix -- people who are trying to control the split of dollars between the various media types. However, there is one thing that advertising does and will continue to do better than anything else: Advertising can drive a company's vision or at least capture the vision in a way that people can embrace. By definition, advertising has to be extremely simple and clear. We take enormous quantities of data and we turn it into 27 words in a TV spot or three words in a tagline, and that has to represent the essence and the possibilities of a brand in a consumer's life. If you write a direct marketing piece, it's got copy – a lot of copy. If you write a press release, it has a lot of words, and then the media picks up on it and editorializes on it. If you do something on the Internet, it has all kinds of different elements. In advertising, you are forced to simplify down to the core essence of what the idea is and why it's important to you. That is extremely critical. You look to leaders to say where they are going and what it is all about. If the leader delivers a page, you're lost. If they deliver a sound bite or the right sentence, you know exactly where you're headed. That's what advertising can do. That is why in many cases advertising is the thing that captures the vision of a brand and then becomes an expression of it, and you will find a lot of other communications unifying under that thought and identity.

Looking to the Future

The real killer app for advertising will be when our business can think seamlessly across communications disciplines and has people who can apply knowledge along the continuum of communications vehicles and techniques (advertising, direct mail, interactive, and public relations), and execute them aggressively. That's the killer app because that's where you figure out how to make all the connections and communications to a consumer, how to build a brand, and how to maximize the return on investment as measured by sales.

From an organizational perspective, we need to create a culture that enables things that, while all under the banner of communications, are genuinely different and require different expertise and competencies but serve a common goal. While these things are different, when you look at them as functional entities, tools and competencies, they all help accomplish a grand-scale vision or opportunity. You can talk about collaboration, but the goal is to build an organization where, at a conceptual (values or philosophical) level seemingly disparate things build a very strong brand in a marketplace. As a weak analogy, we talk about teams. Teams are what accomplish things, not individuals. Within a team, are disparate processes, mindsets, types of people, and organizations that can bring those differences together and enable them not only to coexist but actually flourish and be respected.

In terms of types of advertising, there may come a time when the 30-second commercial is not as prominent, but I don't think it will be totally obsolete. There is some point at which the mind can't absorb any faster than that, so I wouldn't be prepared to call it dead.

There was a time when we'd talk about people who grew up during the MTV generation. That means, of course, that they are used to fast television, rapid interaction and dialogue, with more clutter on the screen, which may seem disjointed to someone used to a more traditional, linear style of conveyance. Look at how that has spilled into the rest of our television, and how the baby boomers now watch television the same way. You cannot turn on cable TV without seeing four different banners. You have the ticker tape along the bottom, the banner, the logo of the program you're watching, and now the latest thing: a vertical bar running along the side. We all absorb communications that way, and it's very interesting. So something that started in a particular age group has infiltrated the entire medium.

We are going to continue to evolve. Two possibilities could emerge, and perhaps both will become reality. One is that when communications and advertising companies really learn how to absorb and support the totality of communication – everything from brand development to transactional-based activities (e.g., customer relationship marketing, online, direct marketing,) – when they can embrace that entire scenario and it can be driven by one vision, the role of advertising can be very different. It does not necessarily have to generate the sale. It may only need to create a feeling and an attachment to a brand that's very emotional. So the question is, could that be done in 15 seconds? Yes, if my purpose is to create an emotional attachment and I don't have to get into a long description of what the product is, how it fits into your life, and how you use it. If I can say to you that I have a communications organization that can do everything from creating that emotional bond to giving you all of the rational information you need and also do the customer relationship management piece, I may be liberated to do that. There's a scenario where you could say that over the long run, there won't be as many 30-second commercials. We just won't need them because we'll have other options. Think about the people watching television and being on the Internet, and a 15-second commercial on TV that's a spear through the heart and creates love and passion – that drives you to a site where you can do all the rational stuff you want. Then the story can be finished. Can it be done in 10 seconds? Maybe. We need people to think that way. That's a scenario that would say it's possible that the 30-second spot could become a thing of the past, and it's not commonplace anymore. The norm has become the exception.

The other direction we could go is back to an old technique. If TiVo and things like that offer an effective way to take the sponsors out of paid promotion, and we can't find our way around them, we may be going back to a sponsored program type of an environment. The advertising entities would become more integrated into the actual program itself, appearing more like the GE Theater.

I think both of those are real possibilities, depending on a variety of things, including an agency's ability to express itself across the entire spectrum of communications tools and being able to manage it properly; the ways technology could facilitate that is also important.

Another area needs to evolve. In order to think outside silos, an agency must create a new breed of thinker. There are no farm clubs for these people. We're doing that every day ourselves. By being inventive, creative and thinking beyond traditional boundaries, we start to teach new people coming into the business that they don't need to be restricted by something on TV, in print or online: any of those things are on our palette of tools. You also need clients to develop in the same way because many clients, larger ones especially, buy in segregated ways. You can only sell a mutual fund to someone who's prepared to buy or understands the purchase of a mutual fund. Years ago, you couldn't sell a mutual fund to someone who only understood the concept of a stock. The buyer has to be in sync with the possibilities. I believe that will happen, and both agencies and clients are moving in that direction.

Joe Grimaldi is president and CEO of Mullen Advertising (Wenham, Mass.), one of the top 25 agencies in the US. For over 19 years, Grimaldi has been a key figure in defining, shaping, and building the Mullen brand. During his tenure, the agency has grown from 14 people and $7.5 million billings to a $640 million agency with 550 people in four offices. It became part of IPG in 1999.

Throughout this evolution, the company has retained its strong culture and distinguished product and reputation. Today, Grimaldi directs agency strategy and development, maintains proactive involvement with clients and accepts ultimate responsibility for total agency operations.

The Future of Advertising:
Merging with Entertainment

Mike Toth

Toth Brand Imaging

CEO & Chief Creative Director

Establishing Brands

For a client to differentiate its product in the marketplace, one must begin with the vision of the brand. We call it brand DNA – the unique qualities or the essence of the brand. It must be determined in advance and relative to its position in the marketplace. Decide whether you want to play in a crowded field or distinguish yourself within that field. Those are strategic issues that are determined early on in a marketing relationship with the brand management team. The next step is understanding what makes the brand different. For example, distribution could be different – channels, pricing, quality, the way it's delivered. You can use many variables to distinguish yourself from the competition, and it's imperative you do so. After you look at the competitive landscape, realize the high ground – a position that's defendable and a place you can create strategies to win.

With all the different media through which a message can be driven, having one consistent message is critical. It's important to have consistency in all messages and all consumer touch points. Consistency, familiarity, reliability – these are the elements upon which a relationship of trust is built. Trust is created through consistency, through delivering on what's expected. That doesn't mean it can't be fresh, and it doesn't mean it has to be predictable. But it still has to be relevant, who you are, and consistently portrayed. When you think about your trust level with people, it comes out of really knowing them and having an idea of what to expect, but that doesn't mean they're going to say the same thing every day.

They have the permission to explore the boundaries within who they are and maintain relevance throughout time. Never abandon who you are because of the lure of the sirens.

Advertising should portray the company's vision. The horse is the vision of the organization and the buggy is the advertising, or maybe even one of the wheels. It's not the whole thing. Advertising doesn't drive an organization; the organization drives advertising.

Challenges of Advertising

Unlike a lot of other marketing tools, advertising allows you to talk to many people very quickly. And provided that message is something people need or want to hear, it can change their lives or make them feel better about themselves. It's an immediate medium. The problem is there are many people who have used the medium to create an instant relationship with consumers and have failed to deliver on the promises – they've lied about the benefits. The result is a cynical consumer whose trust has been broken and whose faith in advertising has become jaded. Ultimately, brands are about trust.

It has gotten more difficult to establish a brand because there are so many more brands vying for attention. The number of companies vying for consumer attention is extraordinary. The stakes are extraordinary. You once could fit in the supermarket, in one-tenth the space, all the brands out there.

Now these huge super-supermarkets are creating more choices. How do you inform consumers about which choices are right for them, and how do you connect with the consumer, and where? The products themselves have expanded and the competition has expanded – and the competition for actually finding a client or a consumer has expanded. So the establishment of a brand becomes more and more difficult.

Assessing risk is another challenge. It's difficult to forecast the success of advertising because you really can't tell what's going to work and what isn't. But you can use some techniques and some research to gain insight. Those companies willing to take risks are the companies more easily able to separate themselves from the competition. Because if you do what everyone else is doing, what is expected, what has been historically proven to work, it doesn't necessarily mean you're going to differentiate yourself. So there are risk-adverse companies, and there are companies that embrace risk, some who've been able to break through and create something extraordinary, such as Phil Knight and the way he has built the Nike brand.

Measuring the return on your advertising investment is a challenge, but there are a number of ways it can be done. One of them is a brand awareness study and what comes to the consumer's mind when the brand is first mentioned. If the purpose of the advertising is either to inform or change then it's critical to know what you're trying to accomplish. You determine what success should look like in advance and then determine what people are thinking, then return to the initial stages and you do the research again.

However, it's beneficial to evaluate it with the understanding of what your definition of success is and why you're investing that money. Is it to increase sales? Is it just to let people know that the brand exists? There are many different ways of defining a successful campaign, but before you begin investing in a campaign, it's good to know how you're going to measure the success. So, you sit down with the client before doing any work and gain a clear understanding of what they're hoping to accomplish.

New Trends

Advertising has become much more focused; it's become a visual shorthand. Ads have less copy. Almost anyone can write pithy headlines, and most advertising agencies are run by creative directors that began as copywriters. In the last couple of years – maybe since September 11 – there's been a return to core values and the things that matter most.

In the future, I believe advertising will merge with entertainment. The power of the emotional chords entertainment taps into – those strands within each of us – will be combined with more of what Hollywood produces. We're going to see increased involvement between production companies and agencies, and in the future the brand will become the show: starting with the profusion of product placement and the impact it's having. Consider the new James Bond picture, for example. It's extraordinary. And it's growing; advertising is going to become part of entertainment. Another example is the more than 200 television channels we now have. In the old days it was just three networks, and now half of the cable channels (or more than half) are run without advertising, and they're commanding extraordinary viewership. If you look at what's going on at HBO with *The Sopranos* or *Six Feet Under*, people are tuning in, and there's no advertising time. Brands are making their way into the fabric of these shows, primarily through product placement, and this I believe will be the new paradigm in the advertising industry.

In terms of new technology, you can now create your own media center online; you can deliver great experiences, welcome people and have a more intimate relationship with them. But we're only in the second inning with the Internet. It is an immensely powerful tool, and when broadband becomes the way of life it's going to open up a lot of doors and give those who otherwise didn't have huge budgets the opportunity to tell people who they are in a quick, compelling way. That won't happen for another few years, when people can gain access to high-speed data input through broadband, but it will be extraordinary. It will change the way we live our lives.

Another interesting development is the group of people who have gone under the radar and done street advertising. Using public relations, and for very little money, they have been able to get into the minds of the influencers within various social groups. As a matter of fact, that's the only way to actually infiltrate some of these really cool groups – through their leaders, and the leaders aren't going to take something they feel has any sort of mass appeal. They're going to take something they've discovered. They're going to actually bring it in and adopt it early on, and then it gets played out to the rest of the consumers as it works its way to the multitude.

Succeeding in Advertising

One of the main keys to successful advertising is a really sound understanding of the role it plays in business and the relationship it has to basic business principles. Advertising is a small part of a very large solution, of helping to add value to an organization. Having the business underpinnings and understanding the role advertising plays is critical. Other important skills are understanding the target audience and their needs, and how the products you're marketing can help them, enrich their lives, or be the solution to a problem.

Most advertising is done in a vacuum, often to support enormous egos, but it's more effective to take ego out of the equation and just see things as they are – as opposed to how we want them to be or how the client thinks they should be. So there is an enormous amount of honesty that needs to be involved in any evaluation or decision.

A lot of the art in advertising involves taste – and advertising is an art, because you're dealing with creative and being able to evaluate things on an artistic/emotional level as well as on an intellectual level. You have to be open and cognizant of what makes something tasteful or not, or what's cool or not cool. You can satisfy all the prerequisites of any campaign once you sit down and decide what it needs to accomplish. But there are many different ways in which that can be solved, and choosing the right one is the art of advertising.

If you want to be successful, it's important to be yourself. Don't try to be something you're not, because the consumer can sniff out a phony. Another key is that it's about not being elite; it's about embracing mass America for the juggernaut it is. Never underestimate the consuming public.

We have a little saying here: "Do good work. God's watching." It means having a conscience about doing the right thing and making sure the client understands we're doing the right thing: People in the organization know we're committed to doing the right thing. We also have what we call "forethoughts," which are four keys to success: know the consumer, know the client, think of things through the client's eyes, then anticipate problems and be prepared to address them.

From a college football player to creative director behind one of this century's most successful branding stories, Tommy Hilfiger, Mike Toth has led a diverse life. Raised in Texas, Toth graduated from the College of the Holy Cross earning a B.A. in Fine Arts. A varsity football player, Toth was named an All East middle linebacker in 1975.

After graduation Toth moved to Paris to pursue a career as an artist. In 1977 on a flight back to the United States, a fellow passenger offered him a job in the ad department of a New Orleans-based apparel manufacturer, Wembley Industries (now Wemco). He spent a year traveling the United States with the sales team, building and breaking down presentations for road show demonstrations company salesmen presented to store buyers. This experience amounted to what he describes as "a master's degree in branding and the elements that create commerce."

In five years later Toth amassed a collection of awards and in 1982 opened his design studio in New Orleans. One of his first clients, named J. Crew at Toth's suggestion, earned national acclaim by presenting the first lifestyle catalogue – a groundbreaking concept that defined the J. Crew brand, restructured the catalogue business and established Toth's reputation as one of the most creative, image-oriented design agencies in the country that specializes in defining American lifestyles.

Toth supports the Fresh Air Fund, offering the organization pro-bono creative services, and advocates for the Special Olympics. In 1984, Toth moved his headquarters to Concord, Massachusetts.

How Advertising Works: Common Sense & Clarity

Ron Berger
Euro RSCG MVBMS Partners
CEO

Art or Science?

The question of whether advertising is an art or a science is often debated. The answer is that it's a combination of both. The art lies in the ability to create a beautiful picture or photograph that has a selling proposition in it. The art also lies in the ability to take a strategy and frame it in a photograph or television commercial.

The science, or business, involves all the methodologies marketers use to measure the effectiveness of communications, including sales, of course.

The most basic skill needed to create an advertising campaign is to write copy, design the look of an ad, and get it executed in a magazine, in newspapers, or on television. The essentials in advertising are a combination of common sense and clarity. As someone once said, common sense isn't common enough in advertising: You always must remember that the people your ads are talking to are your wife, your kids, and your mother-in-law. So it's critical to keep the message simple and clear. Too much advertising sounds like marketingese. There are also a few pitfalls to watch out for. Stupidity would be one: stupid ideas, overcomplicated strategies, or self-indulgent executions of advertising that don't show understanding of what a brand is all about are an enormous waste of time and money.

The difference between advertising and other types of marketing is that advertising allows you to reach many people quickly and to get your message out in the specific way you want. This is different, for example, from public relations where the media messages are unpaid and therefore can be changed or diluted by the reporter writing the story. If you run one commercial on the Super Bowl, a lot of people will know who you are. If it's the right message, if it's interesting and relevant, you'll communicate effectively with your target audience. If it isn't, you'll waste an enormous amount of money. Advertising is very efficient. It can sell everything from cars to hamburgers to Presidents of the United States. If you want to run for political office and have a lot of money, by the end of next week many people will know who you are. And by the end of the first Tuesday in November, you will know how many people have liked what you have had to say and "bought" your product.

Success can be measured in many ways, but it's critical that the role of advertising be understood before you can decide on how success will be measured. The bottom line has to be the amount of products you sell. You want the advertising campaign to drive business in a measurable and hopefully profitable way. In some corporate advertising, the role of advertising is to drive the image ratings of a company or its brand, but even that is usually quantifiable. There should be absolute accountability for the money being spent.

To succeed in advertising, you need to have a smart, simple strategy and a clear understanding of your audience. You need to articulate clearly and create and execute an idea that motivates people in ways they never would have imagined being motivated. And then you need to pray that you're right.

Building a Brand

To build a brand from scratch, you need a deep understanding of its core values. What does the brand stand for? What does it believe? Does it have a compelling idea – a reason for being? Hopefully, that reason for being is different from that of its competition. You also need smart people to take the values and attributes of the brand and articulate them in a way that clearly differentiates them in the marketplace. And you need to do that in interesting, fresh ways over a number of years. Volvo's core value, for example, has always been about putting people before cars. That is why Volvo focuses so deeply on safety leadership in building its cars; it also shows concern for the environment and the world as a whole. Volvo's tag line, "For life," captures the company's core values perfectly.

Going from nothing to an established brand doesn't happen quickly, and many lessons can be learned from dot-com companies: It's nearly impossible to build a brand in just a few months. In trying to do so, many dot-coms failed miserably, and many advertising agencies should have known better. They took the money these companies dangled, but branding just doesn't happen that simply. Even the companies with high-visibility commercials failed. You don't start with a Super Bowl commercial: You start with a business idea and a set of values. Those values and attributes have to have relevance to the audience with which you want to communicate.

Successful brands all have a clear business and marketing strategy. A brand's tone of voice comes out of that strategy and allows the brand to communicate consistently: It looks and feels constant over several years even as it continues to grow. For example, Nike has had a clear tone of voice for a number of years even as it evolves. Consumers recognize that and know Nike stands for a different set of values, human achievement, and not simply for athletic shoes or apparel. This is very different from brands that try to hit "home runs" and breakthrough all the time. The mentality of breaking through has people trying to do things that might be one-shot wonders, like a firework that goes up and crashes down again. There is no shortcut for building a brand that will endure.

The Need to Change

People's lives today are changing in rapid, dramatic ways that we could only dream of a few years ago. The role brands play has to change along with that. To take a brand to the next level, you need to deepen your understanding of the target audience: how their lives and needs are changing. You must continue to develop the product and enhance its attributes so it remains in line with consumers' lives. Smart marketers recognize how people's lifestyles are changing and are constantly looking for ways to make sure their products and communications continue to be relevant. Strong brands can survive forever if they continue to understand and adapt. But to do that, several things must happen. You can never take for granted that what made you successful will continue to make you successful, but you should always know why it made you successful. You need to understand how the marketplace has changed and continue to develop products that deliver on that understanding. This is not to say you should totally reinvent the brand, because that causes confusion. People don't care enough to stay with weak brands or inferior products. They don't have the time to follow brands that keep changing what they are.

The enormous turnover in management is one of the big problems in business today. A new CEO or marketing director comes in, begins questioning what has been done, and changes the marketing focus of the company. That lack of consistency can be very dangerous and damaging to strong brands.

Here is an amazing statistic: Something like 53 percent of the Fortune 500 companies that existed in 1983 aren't around anymore. That's right, more than half of the biggest, most powerful companies in the world just 20 years ago aren't around today. But they have been replaced. Look at how we all live out lives today. We buy our coffee at Starbuck's, our clothes at Banana Republic, our books at Amazon. Home Depot, Staples, Circuit City: Name a category and it's likely that a brand that didn't exist 15 or 20 years ago is dominating our everyday lives. Why? The people who created these brands understood how our lives are changing and developed products, marketing and advertising that made them an essential part of people's lives.

Just Around the Corner

Technology has brought significant change to the advertising industry. The Internet enables us to do something dramatically different and tremendously important that we otherwise wouldn't have been able to do: to have a two-way conversation with consumers. A television commercial is a one-way conversation; it's the brand talking to the consumer. The Internet allows us to engage in a dialogue with people who are interested in having that conversation. We can ask if you're interested in more information on product A, and by telling us you are, you're inviting a conversation. That's a tremendously important and valuable tool that wasn't available a few years ago. But it needs to be understood as just a part of the marketing plan. It doesn't replace traditional media, but it is a powerful tool that smart marketers are using more and more.

The role technology plays will continue to drive changes in our industry, because it's going to continue to drive changes in people's lives. What will be developed in terms of mobility and technology will bring to life a way of living and working that, until now, we've only heard and read about. Intel, for example, is introducing a new generation of wireless technology that will allow us to do virtually anything, anywhere: in effect, to unwire our lives. It's not science fiction. This will happen. It will affect all industries. As a result, the way we communicate with people and what we communicate about has to change as well.

In addition to the technology-related changes, the advertising industry has changed its focus. It has become more about the business of advertising than the advertising business. As more agencies have been consolidated into publicly held companies, too much of the discussion has been about a holding company's forecasts, earnings, and profits. It is understandable but has changed the focus from the quality of the work we do to the quality of the earnings we report. It's a significant shift that began a few years ago. The impact has been that people within the industry – certainly creative people – have lost a little of the magic and also their passion for what advertising can be. It's now about the bottom-line profit more than the craft of what we create. It hasn't affected clients as much: They work for businesses and are accustomed to having to report earnings. Within agencies, it's a more recent phenomenon. Most of the consolidation has happened, so chances are that trend won't accelerate any more than it has in the last few years. Hopefully in the next few years we will find a happier balance between the quality of the product that agencies deliver to clients and the ability to deliver what shareholders need.

Even with this focus on the bottom line, I think we are living in a tremendously exciting time where, more than ever, clients need what great advertising people have always delivered: big powerful business ideas that can drive businesses in dramatic, profitable ways.

Ron Berger has been in the advertising business since age 18 when he took the summer job of mail boy and center fielder for the old Carl Ally agency.

In the 13 years Berger worked there, he won hundreds of awards. His most widely acclaimed work, the "Time To Make The Donuts" campaign for Dunkin' Donuts, was honored by the Television Bureau of Advertising as one of the five best commercials of the 1980s.

In 1986, Berger co-founded the agency that became Messner Vetere Berger McNamee Schmetterer Euro RSCG. The agency was the fastest growing major agency in the advertising industry, boasting a client roster of the world's most forward-thinking companies. As founding partner and chief creative officer, Berger was involved in some of the most memorable campaigns of the past decade. His commercial for Volvo, entitled "Survivors" was selected "Best Commercial of 1993" by Advertising Age.

In recognition of his work, Berger was featured in the Wall Street Journal's Creative Leader campaign.

Named chief executive officer of MVBMS Euro RSCG in 1999, Berger continued to lead the agency's innovative approach to advertising. Overseeing a $1.3 billion dollar agency, he also was named chair of the Creative Committee *for the American Association of Advertising Agencies. He sits on the advisory board of the Children's Health Fund and the Creative Review Committee for the Partnership for a Drug Free America.*

Berger recently completed co-directing and co-producing a feature-length documentary entitled "The Boys of 2nd Street Park," shown at the 2002 Sundance Film Festival and slated to air on Showtime.

With the creation of Euro RSCG MVBMS Partners in 2002, Berger began the next evolution of his leadership, leading a dynamic new Agency that offers Creative Business Ideas™ across all marketing disciplines to a wide array of top brands.

Assessing Good Creative:
$10 of Value for Every Dollar Spent

Stan Richards

The Richards Group

Principal

Successful Branding and Advertising

We define a brand as a promise. It is a promise that there will be certain deliverables that come from this product or service or company, and those deliverables must reach the ultimate consumer at every point of contact every time – otherwise a brand gets weak. The difference between weak and strong brands is consistency. Delivering on a promise at every point in time and opportunity makes a strong brand. To make a weak brand strong or a strong brand stronger, we must understand what the essence of the brand is – what that promise is – and deliver that consistently and effectively. It does not just stop with advertising: It has to find its way into every point of contact with the consumer. An example would be our work for Motel 6. In all of our radio advertising we use Tom Bodet as the lead character, and if you stayed at a Motel 6 and you requested a wake-up call, your wake-up call would not be what you would get at other hotel chains. Your wake-up call would be Tom Bodet, who says something like, "Good morning! You have just won the lottery! Just kidding – but it is time to get up and hit the road." It is that kind of consistency along every point of contact that makes strong brands stronger.

It is important for clients to understand that the greatest risk is being invisible. We have to find ways of making people notice our work. We want to make the work likeable. We want the viewer or the reader to like the advertiser. It is exactly the same as if you were selling in a retail environment – in a car dealership, for instance. If you walked up to a customer as he or she entered a show room, stuck out your hand and said, "Hi. How can I help you?" the very first thing you want to happen is to have that customer like you. I think advertising works in exactly the same way. We try to make our work as endearing as possible – to find some basis on which the viewer or reader will like the work, consequently like the advertiser and ultimately be easier to engage in business. That sometimes involves breaking rules and taking risks, but most often it is simply a matter of putting good work on the table, explaining to the client why it will be effective, and then jumping out and doing it.

Ultimately, what constitutes a successful advertising campaign is moving the needle. Whether this is measured by increasing awareness of the advertiser or enhancing the brand, or whether it is measured at the cash register – both are valid measures of the campaign's success. Success has little or nothing to do with how the work does in the award shows. The ultimate measure is how it works in the marketplace. Are we delivering $10 worth of value to the client for every dollar he spends? That is the difference between weak creative and good creative. Weak creative gives you a dollar's worth of value for every dollar spent. Good creative gives you $10 of value for every dollar spent.

Challenges of Advertising

We deal with an awful lot of information, and it is really important that we have that information in our heads when we sit down to solve a problem. It isn't like being a painter where your only constraint is the size of the canvas; in our case the restrictions become much tighter. We may have an 8½ by 11 page in a magazine we are working with, it may be a full page in a newspaper, or it may be a 30-second TV spot. In any case, we begin with very tight constraints that we have to deal with. We have 30 seconds to capture the viewer's attention and hold it. With print, we have about three seconds. The number of people who will spend the time it takes to read body copy in a print ad is negligible: All readership studies say that, at best, three percent of the people who see the ad will actually read the copy. Basically, what you are getting is the time people will spend to look at a visual and read a headline and then they are on to the next page. The medium with the shortest attention span is outdoor advertising. We are restricted to no more than seven words on an outdoor board because people don't have time to read more than seven words – although we occasionally stretch it to eight or maybe nine. When you look at it in this way, advertising is very different from art as a traditional means of expressing oneself, but it is so exciting and rewarding when you can come up with a solution that does everything a good piece of advertising can do and you've done it within these enormous constraints.

One of the things that can get in the way of doing good work – and this is a significant problem consistently – is dealing with multi-layered clients and the necessity of going through a complicated approval process. Very often there can be as many as five or six approval levels before work actually gets on the air or into print. That is a tedious, dangerous process because the work is often tweaked at every level, and it usually doesn't make it any better. It can be frustrating for the creative person and ultimately an unproductive process for the client. But as most agencies do, we always try to streamline the process, often successfully.

One of Many Tools

Advertising is just one of many tools in the marketing toolbox. It is very important and expensive and therefore it's critical that the marketer gets the most out of it.

Advertising and public relations operate very differently because we control the message in advertising. A good public relations person can cajole a journalist into doing a story but can't be certain the outcome will be exactly how he or she wants it to be. In advertising we have total control: It is a product we can craft and that gives us the opportunity to craft it the way we wish.

Public relations can be highly effective, however, because most people find a positive story about a product or service in the press much more believable because it is a third-party endorsement. There is much to be said for an effective public relations campaign. Direct, interactive and guerilla marketing can also be significant tools under the right circumstance.

Changes in Technology

Technology has changed many things about the way an advertising agency works. We used to do things called paste-ups. When you put an ad together, it went through a paste-up stage, then it was engraved, then it was sent to a publication. Things that took days going back and forth from a typesetter to an ad agency are today done in minutes on a Macintosh where we have a choice of a thousand type faces all available on a moment's notice.

We have an extranet between our office and every client's office. One client, Pergo, a laminate flooring company, came to the United States seven or eight years ago and has been very successful. Pergo's offices and marketing director are in Raleigh, North Carolina and our offices are in Dallas. When we do a shoot – and we do a couple a year – we usually shoot in the Dallas area. We are now at a point where Pergo's marketing director can stay at her office in Raleigh while we set up the shot. When everything is ready, we put a digital camera on the tripod, shoot digitally, send the information through the extranet, and she can say (watching the process on her computer screen), "Yes, I think it's great," or tell us whatever she thinks would improve the shot. Then we take the digital off and replace it with the film camera. We have saved her days of being out of the office. The next step is to do away with film altogether and shoot everything digitally, which is coming very quickly.

As another example, we can edit a TV spot for Home Depot, located in Atlanta, then send that image through the extranet to our client, who can O.K. a rough cut while sitting in his office. Think about the time and costs saved in travel expenses. Things like that happen every day and make us infinitely faster and far better than we were before. Back when we had to edit with film, we would put the film on a Moviola machine, crank it through, and if we wanted to edit we literally took a razor blade and inserted a scene by taping it together. That process took about five minutes. Now that same edit takes three seconds. It has revolutionized the way we edit. We can be much more critical of editing and try things just to see if they work, because there is no detrimental consequence in trying it four, five, or six different ways.

Competition and Quality of Work

We happen to be in an industry where everyone's work is highly visible. It is very easy to see what is going on in the industry. All of us on the creative side spend time with our noses in the annuals to see what is winning awards. It is a constant effort to evaluate our work versus the work of other agencies, and there are a number of opportunities to see that work.

The only important thing, though, is the work. If the work is good, it is good. If you put up the work of half a dozen agencies, you can clearly see the differences. Agencies are always evaluated by their best work. I think it would be better for them to be evaluated based on their worst work, because some agencies do their best work for three to four percent of their clients and at the other end of the spectrum is a vast body of stupid work.

To be successful, the work has to be intelligent; there is no reward for stupidity. Second, the work has to be endearing: People must like it for it to be successful; endearing work must be crafted with great care and attention to detail. The work's intelligence, endearing qualities, and craftsmanship are the most important.

If you are a creative person, you need to focus 100 percent on the work. Don't let anything interfere with the work itself and be passionate about making that work as good as it can be. Be willing to quit a job or resign a client if the work is not up to your standards. You need to develop a sensitive stomach, so that when the work is not what it should be you solve the problem rather than deal with the stomachache.

Stan Richards founded The Richards Group as a freelance practice after graduating from Pratt Institute in New York. Over the next 26 years, it became one of the nation's premier creative resources. In 1976, it became a full-service advertising agency.

Richards' work has received awards in virtually every major competition in the world. In 1976, he was chosen by the Dallas Society of Visual Communications as "the single individual who, over his career, has made the most significant contribution to the advancement of creative standards in the Southwestern United States." In 1981, 1983, 1984 and 1985, Richards was named by ADWEEK as "The Top Creative" in the Southwest. In 1985, The Richards Group was named Agency of the Year. That same year, Richards was honored by Pratt Institute as a Distinguished Alumnus. In 1986, he was honored with an Advertising Age cover story. In 1987, ADWEEK named him "Executive of the Year," and he was included in The Wall Street Journal's "Giants of Our Time." In 1988, 1990 and 1994, the firm was again named Agency of the Year. In 1995, Richards was named an Entrepreneur of the Year by Inc. magazine.

The University of Texas named Richards the 1996 recipient of the Reddick Award for leadership in communication. Previous honorees include Walter Cronkite, Ted Turner and Bill Moyers. More recently, SMU announced the Stan Richards Creative Chair.

Also in 1996, Richards was the recipient of the AIGA Gold Medal, the award for career achievement in design. In 1997, Graphis magazine named The Richards Group one of the 10 best agencies in the world, and the American Association of Advertising Agencies honored the firm with its A+ Award, given annually to America's best agency.

In 1999, Richards received the highest honor available to a creative with his election to the Art Directors Hall of Fame, joining such luminaries as Walt Disney, Norman Rockwell and Andy Warhol.

Apart from business, Richards' interests include skiing in Utah and fly-fishing the backwaters of Laguna Madre. He is an avid runner, having logged 39,000 miles.

In addition, Richards serves, or has served, as a director of The Salvation Army, Episcopal School of Dallas, YMCA, Cooper Aerobics Enterprises, Dallas Symphony Association, United Way, and the Creative Committee of the AAAA.

Active Branding™ :
Combining Branding & Direct Marketing

Christopher Santry

Kupper Parker

President & CEO

The Art of Advertising: Right Brain Thinking?

Many of us who make a living on the creative side of advertising would seem to be right-brain dominant: We rely on instinct, intuition and emotion to a much greater extent than our co-workers in other departments. That is because we are artists. Unfortunately, an advertising campaign is not merely fine art, it's a highly specialized form of communication. If the creative execution has not communicated the client's essential message to its target market, that campaign has failed, no matter how compelling the imagery or how poetic the copy.

The campaign that introduced Infiniti automobiles to the world is a case in point. The campaign was beautifully produced. Each television spot was executed flawlessly to evoke Zen-like feelings of peace and contemplation. But the campaign never communicated the essence of the car itself. As a result, Infiniti's introduction was a financial flop, and to this day Infiniti has been playing catch-up with Lexus (introduced the same year).

The challenge facing all creatives is to harness the emotional power of a campaign as esoteric as Infiniti's introduction and to use their intellectual skills to transform that piece of fine art into a highly focused communication. To exceed the client's needs and expectations of success, creatives must take that extra step.

Two Halves Are Better Than One

If the right brain is the creative center for concepts that will stop consumers in their tracks, the left side of the brain is the intellectual center that can help shape the raw concept into something that demands more of its audience than merely being spectators. Until just a few years ago, it possible to build a brand using only humor, shock or any other creative device that might increase unaided recall. In today's world of instant gratification (on the consumer side and the client side) the old rules for branding no longer apply.

Today, a concept must be crafted in such a way that the consumer feels a more immediate need to interact in some way: whether via the Internet, phone or (in just a few years) the lowly TV remote. And it's not enough merely to tack on a quick graphic at the end of a TV spot. That's where the "left brain" comes in: to take the raw emotion, humor and/or shock value of a concept and focus it into a message that leads the viewer to inevitably act in a way that will satisfy the client's active goals.

This more "whole brained" approach is what it really takes to produce highly creative, yet successful advertising for today's more demanding marketing environment. I even coined a name for it few years ago: "Active Branding," which is described more completely under the heading "The New Math."

Clients Need a Little Respect

Too often, those of us on the agency side seem to brush aside the client's wishes in our quest for breakthrough creative. That old joke "advertising would be a great business if it weren't for the clients" belies an underlying elitism that allows us to be less receptive to valuable client input. That's certainly putting the worst spin on it, but even the slightest bit of "agency attitude" is a tremendous mistake. A better alternative is to assume that a client who has been successful in business has some valuable insights on marketing his or her product. The creative team that goes into a project prepared to listen closely to the feelings and desires of the client and his customers will actually produce a better creative product.

Only when the creative team understands a client's desires can they begin to deal with the client's needs. Otherwise the result may be jaw-dropping but irrelevant. Worse, the resulting campaign will be scorned by the client's own employees.

There was a recent campaign for a national oil heat association whose purpose was to keep oil heat customers from converting to gas heat. The client wanted creative that would make a big impression. What they needed was a campaign based on some solid grass-roots knowledge of how homeowners choose to heat their homes and their relationships with their local oil dealers. The agency produced a spot that depicted a family dressed in clear protective plastic garments, sitting on furniture wrapped in clear protective plastic. This was intended to show that oil heat is clean enough for even the most compulsive homeowners. It was quirky and funny, but it left viewers with the impression that having oil heat means homeowners should wear protective garb in their own homes. The oil heat dealers hated it. More importantly, the message was so poorly conceived that homeowners didn't get it. Needless to say, the account went into review immediately.

Creative vs. Conservative

Based on the above anecdote, one might say that creativity can be very risky, but remember that any process completed without careful study of all the facts will almost always fail.

The question here is if clients are better served by "edgier" advertising. My answer would be an emphatic "yes, but with discipline." If we had more creative ads executed with more discipline, agencies and clients would both be better off. This would be true even if the sociological and technological landscape of advertising had not changed so dramatically in the '90s. It's all the more important if we are to stay ahead of the curve for the next wave of changes, which are just around the corner.

The fact that ad agencies and clients can seldom agree on what constitutes "creative risk" makes this more complicated. The definition of "high risk" by the respective parties is often reversed by 180 degrees. Agency creatives would say that a too conservative campaign would submerge in the swamp of other mediocre advertising. Clients might say a campaign that is too outrageous will make them look foolish or flighty.

In fact, there is truth in both viewpoints. The only way to execute effective advertising is to develop a dialogue where the agency and client actually listen to each other. There is no simple solution to this "Republican versus Democrat" dichotomy, but a little mutual listening (and discipline by both parties) may actually produce some surprises for getting on the same page. Any campaign that gets approved as a result of creative capitulation over the issue of risk by either the agency or client is doomed to failure.

Creating a Successful Ad Campaign

It is not necessary that an ad campaign be unified across all media. Certainly, many agencies and advertisers have had great success with the philosophy that each medium is so unique it requires the best possible creative, even if it departs from the overall campaign.

It must be acknowledged, however, that a campaign managing to unify the creative for all its media outlets under one cohesive message will possess unbelievably powerful synergies. Accordingly, it seems incumbent on creatives to work harder at that unified message before succumbing to a more "media-specific" approach.

Measuring Effectiveness: The New Math

Traditionally, a campaign was supposed to build awareness by a certain percentage within a certain time period. Benchmarks for sales and unaided recall were established. Goals were set for measurable increases in those areas over a six-month to one-year period. Today, the rules have changed. A campaign is expected to produce a bump in awareness immediately and also a bump in sales, but not just a bump in retail sales. These days it must be via multiple sales channels: retail, Internet, direct by phone and other emerging means of communication.

We are now forced to show a return on investment much sooner than we were as little as five years ago, and no two clients have the same absolute measurement for success. Last year, one of our clients wanted to show an increase in existing sales equal to what was to be spent on media within six months. Another expected a certain number of web visits after one month and a conversion rate of 20 percent immediately after that.

There may be no one measurement for success, but the demands for return on an investment are consistently far greater than they ever were before. Interactivity has made instant gratification seem more attainable. As a result, everything is compressing on itself. Internet use will become a greater medium for commerce than it ever has been. The dot-com nightmare of the '90s will become a dream come true, and ad agencies will have to show returns that are almost instantaneous. It won't be too long before the success of a laundry detergent spot will be measured by its success in creating online issuance of promotional coupons (or even online sales) after just a few days.

Anyone who doubts this only has to look at catalog marketers. Leads are analyzed on a day-by-day basis, as are the percentages of resulting sales. Adjustments and cancellations of media are made weekly. This method of advertising and marketing is being adopted by more major advertisers as consumer Internet use increases on a daily basis.

The demands these clients are making are not unattainable, but it takes an approach that combines branding with direct response advertising. Ad agencies used to keep these two disciplines as far from each other as possible, so there might be two very different campaigns for the same client. The problem with that dualized effort is that it is inherently too inefficient to achieve the results now expected.

In the early 1990s, we started work on a campaign for a New England HMO that did combine the branding effort and direct marketing into one integrated campaign. All television media ran as 60-second spots. The branding message was woven into the direct message in a way that worked well for both. The website was integrated into this campaign as was all print and collateral material. This campaign was so successful and so cost effective, we began to apply this methodology to all our clients' campaigns. After a few years of doing this successfully, we realized this technique was good enough to deserve its own name, so we finally trademarked the term "Active Branding."

Active Branding is a simple methodology. In essence, the concept is to utilize the techniques from branding and direct response respectively that will work for both. It can be limiting, because creatives do not have the luxury of developing a story for 25 seconds then revealing the client's name or product in the last five seconds.

Conversely, the message can't contain the kind of creative elements one might see in an overnight spot for exercise videos. However, we have had results that have justified working with those limitations.

The point is we can accomplish what seemed just a little while ago like the impossible. Interestingly, it was the change in technology and the resulting change in consumer expectations that created the challenge in the first place, and it is the use of the same technology that has provided the solution.

Public Relations: Free Advertising?

There is nothing more powerful or influential than a successful public relations effort. Of course, the thing most likely to result in successful public relations is that the product or service is so new or unique the media will readily publish and/or air the desired message. In such a case, it could be said that the client blessed with such a unique product should rely entirely on public relations.

However, the advantage of advertising is that it is a message controlled and focused by the advertiser, not the media outlet. The importance of this cannot be overemphasized in light of the fickle nature of today's media. In truth, the ideal marketing campaign would consist of an integrated and coordinated effort in both areas.

The major film companies seem to do the best job of integrating advertising and public relations. Their ad campaigns are always accompanied by well-coordinated PR efforts with appearances by the stars and director on national and local programs, promotions involving other companies and background stories published by the print media.

Is There a Time to Reinvent a Brand?

The most successful brands in the world are those whose messages have stayed in touch with the needs and desires of their target markets. I think there has been too much emphasis on reinventing brands. There have been times when brands tried to invent themselves as a solution to sagging sales when the solution was really to be found elsewhere.

New Coke is a good example. Here was a case of Coca-Cola (no pun intended) trying to compete with Pepsi by emulating it. The result was a fiasco. Instead of attracting Pepsi drinkers to a new Coke brand that tasted more like Pepsi, Coke lost part of its own customer base.

Nike established the foremost advertising campaign in our industry, "Just do it," then abruptly changed the campaign to something else when the existing campaign was just hitting its stride.

I think individual egos get involved: "This is a great success story, but if I do something new and different I'll make an even better success and it will have my name on it." Too often we try to reinvent something instead of reinventing ways to expound on a brand and develop a fresher way to keep it going as it has been.

The Energizer Bunny is a great example of how to maintain a solid campaign. That campaign has been in force for 15 years. Instead of reinventing the brand, they reinvented the creative for the campaign and have remained the leader in that category.

Branding and the Internet

The Internet has been around since the 1970s, but it did not have a tremendous impact on the way we advertise and respond to advertising until the end of the 20th century. Today, there is not a print ad, radio spot or television spot without a website somewhere in the message. However, that type of solution to making advertising more interactive is simplistic at best.

Advertising is becoming much more a part of a direct response system. We demand interactivity in everything now, and if you look ahead a few years to where the TV and computer will merge in terms of home use, our whole concept of what constitutes advertising may have to change.

The film *The Minority Report* offered a peek at future possibilities for advertising: Tom Cruise walking by an animated billboard that addresses him by name because the database knows he might be interested in that product; a newspaper updated via the Internet to show breaking news. As futuristic as these things seem now, within a few years we may look back on them and think they were pretty tame. The technologies are already there.

The Internet can already reach us everywhere at every moment of our lives, so it's hard to overestimate the impact it will continue to have in the future. What does that mean for ad agencies? Well, if my survey of current ad agency websites is any indication, it means we are behind the eight-ball as an industry. In my opinion, ad agency websites are generally the least interactive and least interesting on the Internet. This may be a case of the shoemaker who doesn't have time to mend his own shoes. I think it's just plain embarrassing.

What's next?

There doesn't seem to be any end in sight to the changes happening in our industry, and we haven't really begun to deal with any of them.

Within a few years, a news story on television will be instantly downloadable as a detailed article complete with background story. What that means for print news media and its accompanying advertising is hard to say.

Satellite radio will make that medium commercial-free and national. Will it take the place of local radio? Or will it become a medium that will customize its message for each individual listening (with a personal ID chip imbedded in the receiver)?

TiVo is a technology that allows viewers to effectively zap advertising. As of this writing, it is not a huge factor, but it will be in just a few years. Spots that are not viewed are not worth paying for, especially if their effectiveness will be analyzed over a very short-term period. There has been talk of a network with no advertising, just product placement. Personally, I'm skeptical about the long-term success of such a method, unless it makes use of the merger of television and computers. The technology would enable a view to point and click a remote at a sweater worn by an actor. The show would automatically pause, and you would be shown a catalog page from which to choose available colors and sizes, then make an online purchase. You would then return to your show. This may not be a happy view of the future, but it is one that seems likely.

The use of TiVo or a similar technology will enable viewers to design their own networks, with a customized lineup of all their favorite shows to be viewed on-demand. A "Wish List" similar to TiVo's will locate all the shows they want to see any time they want to see them.

Whatever happens, the advertising industry must be more proactive. Solutions that we offer now will better help to shape the future of advertising. Otherwise, it will shape itself.

Christopher Santry founded Christopher Thomas Associates with Tom Petrocine in 1975. Their backgrounds as creatives did not prepare them for the business side of running an ad agency, but CTA grew slowly over the next 10 years, working on a mix of local, regional and small national accounts. By the mid-'80s, CTA had about 30 employees in its Garden City, N.Y. office and was doing a lot more broadcast advertising than most agencies that size.

In 1993, CTA received an assignment from Fallon Healthcare, a New England HMO, to rebuild its brand and generate leads for new members.

The company, which was experiencing attrition of 7 percent per year, experienced a 15-percent increase in membership in the first year of the campaign. Fallon continued double-digit growth for another five years, and also received the No. 1 ranking from both Newsweek and US News & World Report in their surveys of HMOs.

After this success, Santry named his methodology "Active Branding" and the process became a staple of CTA's credentials presentations. Black & Decker Housewares agreed to try Active Branding for a handheld electric can opener called "Gizmo," with results exceeding the previous company record for sales of a single product.

In 2001 Christopher Thomas Associates became a part of the Kupper Parker Communications group under the name KPC Christopher Thomas. Santry continues to serve as senior partner of creative services.